Spirituality and

the Writer

Spirituality and the Writer

A Personal Inquiry

THOMAS LARSON

SWALLOW PRESS / OHIO UNIVERSITY PRESS
ATHENS

Swallow Press
An imprint of Ohio University Press, Athens, Ohio 45701
ohioswallow.com

© 2019 by Thomas Larson
All rights reserved

Printed in the United States of America
Swallow Press / Ohio University Press books are printed
on acid-free paper ∞ ™

29 28 27 26 25 24 23 22 21 20 19   5 4 3 2 1

Library of Congress Cataloging-in-Publication Data
Names: Larson, Thomas, 1949- author.
Title: Spirituality and the writer : a personal inquiry / Thomas Larson.
Description: Athens, Ohio : Swallow Press, 2019. | Includes bibliographical
references.
Identifiers: LCCN 2018056387 | ISBN 9780804012126 (hc : alk. paper) | ISBN
9780804041041 (pdf)
Subjects: LCSH: Autobiography--Religious aspects. | Authorship--Religious
aspects--Christianity. | Authors--Religious life. | Religious
biography--History and criticism. | Spiritual biography--History and
criticism.
Classification: LCC BL71.5 .L37 2019 | DDC 808.06/692--dc23
LC record available at https://lccn.loc.gov/2018056387

To my son Blake
and to the memory
of my partner's son Scott.

Contents

Acknowledgments

First, I offer thanks to the editors of four online publications where the following essays, their material reworked for this book, first appeared in 2017: *Los Angeles Review of Books*, "Leo Tolstoy and the Origins of Spiritual Memoir"; *Berfrois UK*, "Thomas Merton and the Language of Spirituality"; *Pacifica Literary Review*, "The Reliably Spiritual Author"; and *Assay: A Journal of Nonfiction Studies*, "What I Am Not Yet, I Am."

Next, I salute those who joined me for an AWP (Association of Writers and Writing Programs) panel "Writing the Spiritual Memoir" in Los Angeles in 2016: Kathryn Winograd, Janice Gary, Shann Ray, and Beverly Donofrio. I also acknowledge my co-participants on the panel "The Faithful and the Faithless" at the NonfictioNOW conference in Phoenix in 2018: Jessie van Eerden, Jenna McGuiggan, Sarah Beth Childers, and D. Gilson. I appreciate those friends and colleagues who listened to my evolving ideas, especially about the spiritual memoir, and thereby helped me clarify my often-unruly thoughts: Richard Buch, John Christianson, Linda Haas, Rosanna Hardin Hall, Steve Harvey, Richard Keith, Jane Lipman, Joe Mackall, Joan Mangan, Donald Morrill, Suzanna Neal, Jo Scott-Coe, Michael Steinberg, Sandi Wisenberg, and several MFA students at Ashland University who struggled valiantly with their own enigmas while trying to write about religious and spiritual experience.

Last, my deep regard for the crew at Ohio University Press / Swallow Press: director Gillian Berchowitz for wanting the book and wisely suggesting the final chapter; managing editor Nancy Basmajian for taking on more editorial worries about my prose than she deserved; and John Morris for his good-humored and unerring copy editing.

Religious Author, Spiritual Writer

The very best in art is too spiritual to be given
directly to the senses; it must be born in the
beholder's imagination, though it must be
begotten by the work of art.

—*Arthur Schopenhauer*

Most of us in the West know what a religion is. We know it by
its myths and artifacts, its history and beliefs, its God and its
texts. In the Judeo-Christian tradition, we know that old white
man, Jehovah, bushy gray beard and furious scowl. We know John
the Baptist, his sandals in the river, and Francis, the people's pope,
his slippers in the Vatican. We've stood before the Celtic cross and
inside the cathedral of Rheims. We've seen still and moving images
of mitered bishops, snake-handling evangelicals, boy preachers as
young as two. We've imagined a monk praying in a Benedictine
cell, a nun chanting Compline in a convent chapel. We've beheld
Grünewald's *Isenheim Altarpiece* and Titian's *Madonna and Child*.

We've heard Protestant hymns and civil rights anthems, Bach's *Christmas Oratorio* and Leonard Bernstein's *Mass*. In Barcelona, there's the Sagrada Familia. In Rome, St. Peter's Square. At Holy Ghost in Harlem, the Pentecostals roll the holy up and down the aisles, while in Mexico City, pilgrims stream by the Shrine of Our Lady of Guadalupe. The blood of the nailed Christ drips on our upturned heads. Whether it's real or metaphoric doesn't matter; we raise his suffering above all as our Lord and Savior.

Most of us know the Judeo-Christian texts—dictated documents and composed convictions whose pronouncements, parables, and punishments are decreed by God and dispensed by humankind: the Talmudic Law, the Ten Commandments, the Gospels of Matthew, Mark, Luke, and John. And, though not all of us subscribe, most of us recognize religion's brightest beam: to flock a congregation of like-minded souls who share moral convictions, ceremonies of birth, baptism, marriage, and death, as well as obeisance to a supreme being.

As much as we know that a religion is its palpable presence in the world, we cannot claim the same of faith's capricious partner, spirituality. We know that realm—if we do at all—by its immateriality, its expressions inscrutable, transient, and inborn.

Spirit suggests a life force, a will, which Arthur Schopenhauer calls the "striving of matter," the "eternal becoming and endless flux" of life. We don't know for certain, but at one time spirit may have brought dead matter to life, stardust to chemistry. Spirit invites paradox almost from the get-go. Its absence from our grasp is its presence. It's the unseen in the "evidence of things unseen." It's a ghost in the machine. Invisible but charged. Embryonic. Popping in unannounced. Gone in a heartbeat. The spirit-voice of the wind. The spirits in a gin and tonic. The spirt of an imp or a goblin, conjured or cast out. The spirit of our Revolution. The spirit of the 1960s. The spirit of Black Lives Matter. Spirit manifests in singers like Billie Holiday, in towns like Santa Fe, in buildings Frank Gehry designs, in the pinstripes worn by the New York Yankees. Spirit guides the Eucharist, the Day of the Dead, the Quaker meetinghouse, the cradle and the coffin maker. Even without the New Age woo-woo of *The Secret,* most of us know that spiritual feelings are real. Our spirits bend from elated to depressed, from songful to sorrowful. Merciless, we break the horse's spirit; bereft, we sing a Negro spiritual. We laud the men who gave "the last full measure of devotion" at Gettysburg and honor the spirit of those dead men who live on, somehow, if only by reciting Lincoln's matchless address.

It seems impossible to separate religion and spirituality. One reason is that the spiritual, which predates organized faith, has been appropriated, if not colonized, by the fixed doctrines, the pious rites, and the tribal sects that further a creed's cause. Religious pioneers branded the appropriation the *holy spirit,* a divination for members who acquire the creed, by conversion or birth. Untold examples come to mind: the haloes encircling the heads of saints in medieval paintings, the crutch-throwing and money-soliciting circuses of televangelists, the prayers of parents who petition God to save their opiated babies and selves.

In contemporary America, amid a stalled Christianity and an avid New Age, where sects are returning the transcendent to its pagan realm, our culture has little agreement as to what spiritual means. Nowadays, all sorts of hip practices vie for coverage; they are sacerdotal and silly, kooky and generic. Celebrities in particular are the new (and least qualified) purveyors. They promulgate unnuanced notions that spirit is synonymous with sensitivity, compassion, an innate sense of fairness and peace. The spiritual, they say, focuses on love, caring for oneself and others, kindness to animals and the planet. It can also be spiritual to tidy your desk and pack your suitcase well, parceling that transcendent feeling into a diet and exercise program or a Viking cruise. From it we get dubious concoctions like "interfaith ministry," "smiling meditation," "mediumship," "messages from the other side," and "mindful recycling."

In our hothouse environment of uncheckable climate change and mass migration, religious certitude continues to threaten our survival. To see beyond the headlines seems to be good for all beings, who, if nothing else, are or should be or should hope to be humane. Though unlikely, the fundamentalist must lie down with the atheist, not to mention the Muslim with the Jew. We agree Dr. Martin Luther King Jr. was religious *and* spiritual in the best sense. But despite King's grace, religion's tribalist nature, its rare reform, and its right-wing politicization of late encourage the unaffiliated to avow they are "spiritual but not religious."

Many in the West want to reconstitute spirit outside our history's two-millennia tower of Bible-based faith. Indeed, removing the spiritual from the religious—emphasizing that *but not*—is one of the deeper, and least acknowledged, causes of our cultural malaise.

Today, we live in a culture that is severing spirituality from religion. The examples are everywhere apparent. Millions wish to sever spirit from religious sects that inculcate one belief over another. To sever spirit from religious sects who say disbelief in their way is a ticket to hell. To sever spirit from sacred texts whose so-called divine origin argues against science or wars on behalf of the saved. To sever spirit from Christian commandments and the exemptions their adherents claim the U.S. government needs to protect. To sever spirit from all that so what we hope remains is uncorrupted, personal, universal, and kind. Whatever the outcome, spirit has a fierce, renewable, intrinsic value, which we cling to like a life vest.

Religion is put upon us, most heavily in childhood, by parents who maintain it is a right to raise their children in the faith. Once acquired, that faith in most heirs seldom strays from their parents' beliefs and remains immovable like blood. The spiritual, by contrast, strays any way it chooses. It may take you in, take you on, take you for a ride, but just as fickly let you go—for spirit has other winds to hound, other souls to haunt beyond loyalty to family or the prosperity gospel. The spirit is the fairest of fair-weather friends. And there are those who as creators of art and makers of literature activate that fair-weathering without recourse to anything institutional. Most of them—most of us living in the age of *but not*—know that the arts we practice need no religion to shape our inviolable sense of how and who we want to be.

IF THE spiritual need not lie with a faith, might it lie more reliably somewhere else? At times, the spiritual is out there, a heron gliding over the lake, uncageably alone and free. At other times, the heron is caged within, that is, *preternaturally* within, as unfettered as a lion cub. We may call on the spirit and the spirit may refuse. Then again, the spirit may be smitten and leap in, taking his saxophone solo. Erratic turns and misty off-ramps comprise the contemporary character of spirituality. What's more, spirit is a kind of unrehearsed intimacy we have with an unknown—the timelessness of nature you are lofted into at the edge of the Grand Canyon or the helplessness your stomach roils with while stirring your son's ashes into garden soil.

It's from these without us / within us modes of celestial and private being that my inquiry begins. On a seesaw, I go up and down, studying the *inner* stake religious authors and spiritual writers bring to their work. The dichotomy is entirely mine, though I aim to simplify and to extend it. At once, there's the literary parent, the classic autobiography, centuries old. At once, there's the literary descendent, the new American memoir. Autobiography and memoir pedestal personal veracity, from which social and cultural reflection arises.

The spiritual dimension that exists in personal writing has its seed in the formidable convert Augustine, the foremost of confessional authors. His guilt-ridden and shame-based tell-all, *Confessions,* remains the apotheosis of self-disclosure for any of us who write personal essays and memoir.

I'm interested in this field only when the writing is authentically personal, felt, and original, which, as such, increases the likelihood of its reliability and, at times, its truth. How difficult it is to describe the inner experience of our enigmatic selves, how cunningly we *set* or *trouble* our beliefs. Spiritual understanding sets the conduct of our belief, in private and social domains, in lieu of a religion's often single-minded insistence that we ascribe to what the fathers of the faith assert.

Incomparable, epiphanic events in our rainy and sunny lives spring on us nonverbally; it is only when rapture (or dread) is given a tongue to speak, or a literary style to write, does it become real to others. Reality, proof, testimony, take your pick. Textual semblance transforms an epiphany. Words, and their best order, highlight language's evocative and expansive realm, whereas, by comparison, any lived numinous moment fades. In its wake, a new discursive experience arises—*writing*, which itself may be an incomparable, epiphanic event all its own.

Among the questions I'm asking are, How do life-writers express these spiritual breakthroughs? Do their works differ from each other? How might differences be significant for writer and reader? For example, if you write from the Christian faith, what makes the story Christian? What in the literature of Christianity *do* we value—surely not a mere summary of biblical tenets? And what are the pillars of past confessional writing that yield the leafy green and the hanging fruit in the spiritual memoir today?

It seems not to matter whether these life-writers are the guilty disclosers of sin-soaked autobiography or the unruly testifiers of revelatory memoir. In either form, we herald someone like Thomas Merton, the young hedonist who in his twenties converts to Catholicism and ten years later, in 1948, writes his majestic self-examination, *The Seven Storey Mountain*. Merton works with strategies of rhetoric and narration, often in the Augustinian model of depravity and salvation, until he realizes he's telling his story, in part, to reveal and to convince himself how Catholicism has rehabbed him. That's his motivation. And yet, despite his tale's honesty and intensity, he understands that autobiography is not the measure of a man. In a letter to the French philosopher Étienne Gilson, Merton expresses the core idea: "Please pray for me to Our Lord that instead of merely writing something I may *be* something."[1]

Our best spirit-haunted narratives are chockablock with queries about the topsy-turvy relationship between writing and the author's life. Such narratives grow more unwieldy the more each *scriptor*, a useful synonym from Roland Barthes, grapples with those queries. As we will see, Merton's story is a case in point.

For first-person authors, the most germane question to ask is this: To what degree is your art, backboned by your religious or your spiritual quest, your lost or never-lost faith, a voyage of uncovering the mystery of sudden, numinous, and life-altering events, whose tensions and illusions and disclosures will not let you be, until you start writing about them?[2]

BEFORE TACKLING my many questions, I want briefly to examine the origin of writing, the expressive dimension of speech. Speech's domain is the fountainhead of storytelling and the source of language's felt nature. To illustrate, consider the shaman who uses his body to conjure fate, or the charismatic Billy Graham, who testifies that God is as real to him as his skin. So much of their communicative value rests on voice, passion, sincerity, emotional logic, oratorical flourish, and the live, sweating, possessed enactor or taleteller whose conviction is on display. It's called testimony, *Tell it, Brother*: the more animated its theater, the more enthralled are the bodies who receive it.

First order of distinction. Text is not speech. Such was the great insight of those who wrote or took down God's dictation *as* the Bible: in order to make the writing come alive—to a largely illiterate and awestruck audience—disciples had to preach the Word. By contrast, readers have fewer means of verifying the convicted spark when the voice, its arousal, its elegance, its bellow is silenced onto or by the page. As music elicits feeling much more directly than text can, so, too, does the sonority of the heaven-bent pastor elicit faith in and for the community than a treatise on original sin. Better to bloodedly quote Leviticus than to turn in another student essay.

Eric A. Havelock, in *The Muse Learns to Write*,[3] describes "written discourse" as the singular tool that moved us from a wholly speaking culture to a multiliterate one, ca. fifth century BCE. This shift "from Greek orality to Greek literacy" activated the intellect, helped organize thought, developed rules for argument (the source of democracy), and created libraries of knowledge (the birth of hard science). Moreover, Havelock argues that once oral discourse intermingled with written documents in our history, the crossover "represent[ed] a new level of the human consciousness," "which as it speaks also thinks" (114). *As*, as in simultaneously.

In its wake, what proliferated, Havelock says, were new terms "for notions and thoughts and thinking, for knowledge and knowing, for understanding, investigating, research, inquiry." Socrates brought "this new kind of terminology into close connection with the self and with *psyche*. For him, the terminology symbolized the level of psychic energy required to realize . . . what was permanently 'true,' as opposed to what fleetingly happened in the vivid oral panorama." The basic contrast was that speaking retained its hold on "feeling and responding," while writing became the "'true' mental act of knowing" (115).

Writing became indispensable to—if not a mirror of—knowledge.

Despite the transition, speaking retained its virtues: narrative, dialogue, drama, grammatical and rhetorical improvisation, and the first-person voice, "I." For a time, vocal finesse remained true of spontaneous debates among disputants in the Greek agora. Each disputant has a point of view, and that point of view is as real as the in-person voice of its utterance. But imagine the speaker has grown more articulate because he also writes. Writing gives him distance and perspective and circulates his ideas among others; he may become known for his individual *style*. In addition, writing nurtures topicalization, history, reflection, philosophy, and an impersonal "you," a "he," or a "she," which broadens the idea that any "I" might be informed. Here is what many of us regard as worth knowing—a *written* truth based on but often different from what is said. Recall Plato copying and structuring and emphasizing the ideas of Socrates as foundational to Western civilization.

I don't think this oral-written distinction and the oral-written merger is too pat. An oral action implies doing, practicing, performing: the Muses sing, dance, and recite in orgiastic rituals. A *literate* action implies stating, thinking, knowing: as I say, Plato spent his adulthood preserving the ideas of Socrates for future generations to study. Researchers and intellectuals pore over the civilizing juggernaut Greek literacy launched. Though it was a complex shift, the idea is simple: speaking begets writing, and writing, enhanced by the recitation of texts, which, in a sense, is a new way of speaking, begets reading.

How is this relevant to religious and spiritual texts? Declaring a creed, orally or as a scriptor, is the *evidence* of same. According to one American evangelical, "God said it, it's in the Bible, I believe it." Testimony of the speaker differs from the testimony of the writer, of course, although, with the slow-growing authority of a text critical to the speaker's message, those testimonies begin to merge. The goal is to join what was spoken with what is read. The ensuing book has it both ways. Eventually, for example, the Bible's textuality supplants the content of *what is spoken*. The spoken has conquered but the written rules. The spoken cannot be infallible because it can be changed. The text is text for all time.

Confessional writers, churchly and otherwise, testify by stealing or miming or extending the tools of a spoken or acted story. The traits of the hero's myth or tale are everywhere known: a dramatic rising-and-falling narrative, a narrator who guides a character to his destinal end, and a writerly insistence on telling details and vivid metaphors. This is Homer's *Odyssey* and it is the story of Jesus. What's more, if it's the latter, a religious text, it must embody direct messages. For example, Christ's "Whosoever liveth and believeth in me shall never die."

For all that, the best literary writers do something more exacting. They make a person, a mere representation of a woman, say, *live* on the page. Such animation projects and, thus, possesses a self. She shows more than she tells, she personifies more than she illustrates, she eulogizes and schemes more than she syllogizes and deliberates—tricks of the trade the writer animating a character, even if it is her "self," uses to both their advantages.

I THINK it safe to state that when searching for the beginnings of a religious literature, we will find that those beginnings are collective. We read, at times admire, the mouthpieces we know in no other way than via text—Moses and Isaiah, lawgivers, rabbis, and prophets, the vanity-plagued assembler of Ecclesiastes, the gospel writers, Matthew, most magnificent, and Paul, the theological wordsmith. Each fashions his truth claim, via statement and story, in Hebrew, Aramaic, Greek, and Christian script. They nail down these claims on parchment scrolls, which are collected and bound into a book, *the* book, a holy book. The Bible is one prime exhibit—a written mélange of polyphonic and centuries-old views whose leather-bound contents, stitched by hand for lap or hand to cradle, canonize derring-do tales and moral choices into portable, quotable creeds.

Writing a religion becomes the religion.

What's written is scripture—declared by its author (the Lord) or its authors (the scribes) as revealed truth, here John 1:1: "In the beginning was the Word, and the Word was with God, and the Word was God."[4] Note how each succeeding phrase is a rhythmic diminution and how each phrase holds to the anapestic (short/long) stress of "the *Word*," creating cadential closure. The aesthetic turn, a testament to that sentence's composer, kerosenes a literary light and, thus, illumines a bright ore. But as scripture stamps out thousands of these claims, we have a problem. Scripture's aesthetic is displaced. Instead, the fact or evidence of the words—the Word itself—rules, becomes, as I say, unalterable, inerrant. The "Word of God" is fixed, set in stone. We are no longer in the realm of the *writing* but, instead, in the realm of the *written*. (Memoirists know that once your story is written and published, the drama is locked in for good. The degree to which it is factual or exaggerated matters less than its chiseled embodiment in print. The same can be said, in our time, when one's actions are "caught on video.")

Most of us know what scripture is: in the West, it is the Torah and the Bible. For two dozen centuries, books emulate scripture. The apocryphal gospels, Gnostic literature, the Talmud, even the Book of Mormon (1830). There are service books: Catholic catechism and the *Book of Common Prayer* (1549). Theological tracts: *Summa Theologica* by Thomas Aquinas (1274) and *Apologia Pro Vita Sua* by John Henry Newman (1866). Hagiographies and martyrologues: *Lives of the Saints* by Ælfric of Eynsham (997) and *The Lives of the Fathers, Martyrs and Other Principal Saints* by Alban Butler (1759). Devotional books: *Spiritual Exercises of Ignatius of Loyola* (1524) and the *Seeds of Contemplation* by Thomas Merton (1949). And metaphysical verse: *The Temple* by George Herbert (1633) and *Paradise Lost* by John Milton (1667). Spiritual allegories: *Piers Plowman* by William Langland (1390) and *Pilgrim's Progress* by John Bunyan (1678). Mystical how-to's: *Introduction to the Devout Life* by St. Francis de Sales (1608) and *The Four Agreements* by Don Miguel Ruiz (1997). Worshipful prose: Thomas à Kempis's *The Imitation of Christ* (1427) and *The Book of Margery Kempe*, written in the 1430s and considered the first autobiography in English. And, in the New World, personal tests of faith: *The Sovereignty and Goodness of God: Being a Narrative of the Captivity of Mrs. Mary Rowlandson* (1682) and *The Autobiography of Benjamin Franklin* (1791).[5]

The term for scripture's origin is not written but *revealed*. It has arrived, a gift messengered to humankind, sparked by a bush or a skylark or an exaltation of scribes who heard it from on high (or, some say, wrote the revealed words because of God's inspiration). The gift did *not* appear as a symphony, a mural, or an ASCI code, which means, in a nutshell, that texts reign. As I say, religions are nearly all empires bred and disseminated by the book. What other physical evidence do they have?

We arrive at sacred and near-sacred texts, which we know via their lofty tone and annunciatory style. Their journey into book-being is essentially over. However, the journey taken and told by the wayfaring pilgrim is something quite different from scripture. Indeed, an individual testament, by one who walks the Pilgrim's Way in England, for example, avows faith and, on occasion, deepens doubt, a see-for-oneself standard unlike the holy book's "believe it or else" rationale.

When spiritually minded authors take any nonfiction form as their lingua franca, they hope to enact *in language* their relationship with the sublime and the inexpressible or, under a religious aegis, with the ideas of suffering and evil. The degree to which any relationship to the ineffable is true from the writer's point of view may or may not be the degree to which it is true from the religion's point of view. This is a major rub. God's book and God's textual purveyors differ enormously from the pilgrim's tract—as everyman's does from the individual's.

℘

IN THE early Christian era, the Bible authorized thoughts and feelings about the context of faith, say, joy at the pearly gates of St. Peter, wonder about the Magi bearing gifts, horror over Christ's crucifixion. The object of these thoughts and feelings eventually began to change once the reader of the Bible realized that its stories of sin and damnation, hope and glory, were targeting *him*—his doubts, his failures, his devotion.

Oh sin, oh damnation, oh hope of glory other than what this wretched life offers—all this was terrifying enough to bring about the *Confessions* of Augustine, the first, the most fully felt, and the most compelling of life stories. Most felt and compelling because the book centers on the depravity of sin in light of God's love and because of the pathos of Augustine's exquisitely crafted testimony. What Augustine starts in 400 CE still haunts autobiography and memoir, a kind of pox whose scars any tell-all must bear. Even today, our oversharing culture remains fixed on the memoirist's shame. Just one example: Mary Karr, whose 2009 *Lit* describes the pigsty of her alcoholism and the rescue dogs of AA and Catholicism. The book's neurotic power issues from her rattling the reader with tales of binge drinking, of swearing it off, of bingeing again while swearing it off. Karr's testament is much like Augustine's—it takes divine intervention and a feral will for her to realize just how bad off she is.

This book, *Spirituality and the Writer*, maps the trajectory from scripture to confession, from essay to memoir. It lingers on, with aesthetic and critical pleasure, the literary qualities of the old forms as well as their innovative contemporaries.

To get the inquiry going, I present a classic of mystical confession by the sixteenth-century Spanish poet John of the Cross: *Dark Night of the Soul*.[6]

Dark Night is an odd bird. It begins with an eight-stanza, forty-line poem followed by a lengthy treatise analyzing the theology behind the poem. "As we embark on an explanation of these verses," John writes, "the soul who utters them is speaking from a place of perfection" (28). He personifies the soul as *she*, alternating her voice with his. (Arcane Christian narratives denote the soul feminine, God, masculine.) Like the stalker Glenn Close in *Fatal Attraction*, the she-soul is "so on fire with love for God that she will get to him by any means necessary" (17).[7]

What's so striking about this tract is how scant John's actual story is. His biography comes from other sources. During the Spanish Inquisition, John was identified as a Catholic "reformer." His and other orders, including the "Barefoot Carmelites" of Teresa of Avila, sought a return to monastic simplicity, unmediated aloneness with their savior. As monastics, they were rebelling against papal ecclesiastics who demanded total submission to church rule. In 1577, John, captured by friars in Toledo, was held nine months in a six-by-ten cell which, before his incarceration, was used as a communal toilet, and where he existed with inadequate food, light, warmth, and clothing. He was taken out only to be flogged while the monks ate their dinner, and where, internally, as translator Mirabai Starr reports, "over time the divine presence began to fade" (5–6).

But John, the post-captive, hardly sounds as if he's in prison. In *Dark Night*, there is poetry—the initial poem, "Songs of the Soul," steams up the windows and reflects the torrid elopement of the she-soul and her Beloved, God. Their passion, an interior swoon, eroticizes the dark: "O night, that guided me! / O night, sweeter than sunrise! / O night, that joined lover with Beloved! / Lover transformed in Beloved!" (24).

Elsewhere we find that what John endured has been depersonalized in the writing. Which may mean that God prefers us in our representativeness, not a one-to-one dynamic. What John suffered—no doubt, roach-ridden insanity—is almost all accounted for in esoteric argot. Here's one of many such servings in Starr's able rendering.

> God cherishes the soul's absence of self-satisfaction and her sorrow in not serving him. This means far more than any of the spiritual pleasures in which she used to indulge, and more than any of her religious doings; no matter how lofty they have been, these deeds were the occasion of many imperfections and unconsciousness. Innumerable blessings flow from the fountain that is the source of self-knowledge to the soul that is humbly clothed in the cloak of aridity. (76)

John's book is Christianly therapeutic, to be sure. Here's how the soul should progress, though I'm not sure how removing the "cloak of aridity" will let the "innumerable blessings flow." Its oddity is that it *sounds* spiritual, but abstractly so. There is precious little of the palpable, tortured, befouled, hungry, boil-racked body to convince us of the corporeal chord it claims to be *sounding*.

IN OUR time, New Age culture (Mirabai Starr is one exponent) has appropriated "dark night" to mean spiritual pain, which is necessary to personal healing. But for John, in 1577, that end does not apply. He plies metaphor, which, mimicking a mystical affair, results in sense-obliterating nothingness, a kind of suicide of the self. The union he wants with the divine is humanly unattainable: "A soul only achieves perfection," John writes, "in proportion to the perfect habits she has cultivated" (36). The she-soul describes the many ways in which you, a perfection-adept, *won't* last the "dark night." The chief roadblock is to assume you're more spiritual than you are. If you're on the quest, you're already handicapped by pride, greed, lust, anger, envy—emotions that distract you from the soul's mission. Much of the she-soul's exposition tells how you'll fail, how ego abrades your spirit, how your senses mislead you, how questions weaken your compliance. Indeed, "only a few souls ever pass beyond the night of sensory purification" (84).

The chaste contemplatives of John's Carmelite Order try and dissolve the ego, so longing falls and spirit rises. There's a process. Initially, one shuts off the body's senses, its "false self." During John's first night, "the soul is stripped of all *perceptions* of God." In the second "night of spirit, all *ideas* of God fall away" (italics are *not* added). God, happy you've dumped your vanity, now unites your interior with his command to banish the self. "Apprehending the word of God" via John's way means "the soul becomes acutely aware of her own insignificance" (75). The soul then possesses a designified "I"—the goal of Christian mysticism, medieval or modern. You are purified, voided. You achieve a kind of feelinglessness, or no-mind.[8]

In John's descriptive flurry, it's unclear how you purge your core desires. Taking this path, your soul must feel excruciating pain. Just as the body does. An existential question is piqued: How would we know the soul's emotions except as those emotions braise our skin or fray our nerves? Starr advises: "By sitting quietly with the breath, the blessed 'no-self' begins to emerge" (13). Set aside *how* this is done, sixteenth-century-style. If one annihilates "I," what's left to feel *the spirit with*?

One of John's goals, it seems, is to resurrect the soul, abandoned in our prelapsarian past. To get there, he warns, beware "the path of the mind." "Discursive thought and imagination" derail the soul's advancement. (So much for memoir.) The goal is "formless prayerfulness," that is, "doing nothing." Being over becoming. John's purpose is to focus "loving attentiveness" on God. That's all that matters.

Dark Night portrays what is personally inconceivable, not what is demonstrable. It is the spiritual equivalent of praying away cancer, which generations past labeled "faith healing" and current practitioners now call "spontaneous remission." Today, we judge John of the Cross's discourse as a metaphor for becoming as "empty" of ego as the divine (presumably) is. And yet to locate God in this way cannot be *redescribed*—the no-self has no self (pardon the hocus-pocus) with which to report the obliteration it took to locate God.

Even Catholic sticklers, heeding the doctrine of original sin, discount this putative union between God and the writer, or the artist for that matter. Under "Mysticism" in *The New Catholic Encyclopedia,*[9] we learn that our means of "experiencing" God is incompatible with the "sense experience" that defines us and, certainly, defines human creation.

> Since any created nature is finite and liable to imperfection, only by special divine help would human nature be able to abide permanently in the enjoyment of a situation calling for the complete integration and subordination of all its faculties to the purposes of the spiritual side of its being. Having lost that preternatural endowment, man, of himself, is no longer capable of that intellectual awareness of God which, if awareness is to be adequate, must obviously be free from the distorting effects of imagery. God is pure spirit and is therefore not to be described in language drawn from sense experience. (113)

In "The Rhetoric of Scripture and Preaching," Carol Harrison notes that for some Christians literature is yet another polluted runoff *proving* the Fall of Man: "Adam and Eve enjoyed a direct and intuitive grasp of the truth in their minds and had no need for language to convey, or mediate it, for them." Language, she continues, "to some extent, is a result of the Fall: it forms a veil which obscures, distances, hides the truth from fallen man, whose eyes are no longer able to gaze upon its brightness. It separates and distances one man from another; it is essentially arbitrary; it can dissemble, misrepresent, be misunderstood."[10]

Writing, painting, sculpture, music, film, are "drawn from," if not "drawn to or by," our "sense experience." But despite that magnetic pull, the arts, so the authors of "Mysticism" claim, distort the pure spirit of God. Though it's arguable whether the spirit of God and the spirit of the arts are comparable, it still seems the paradox is joined: Christians tout the Bible's Word of God as inerrant, but any Word distorts God's pure spirit.

What do we do with this and other paradoxes? Abandon them? Reconcile them? Leave them irreconcilable? Why did Augustine, Teresa of Avila, Thérèse of Lisieux, Thomas Merton, and a few other literarily called authors unpack so eloquently and so lustily these distortions and contradictions if only to show us that language itself may also, like the soul, house the mystery of existence?

One bad result of all this: such conundrums embarrassed clerics and led them to sanitize or censor writers for millennia. Anyone who appealed to the purely sensual aspect of the reader the church editors targeted as gratuitous, immodest, vain. One argument has been that God doesn't need the sentiments of anyone's ego because none holds a candle to his. So, the critic asks: Why does God need so much praise, so much worship, even written confessions that testify over and again to his perfection?

Thus, we've been encumbered with a tradition of devotional autobiographers who, like John of the Cross, adhere more to the pontifical, less to the experiential. These books, as we'll see, advocate collective or sanctioned schemes and tropes, rarely exhibit a tangy style or a sultry voice. They fall into habits of toady sentimentality, eschew the irreverent pungency of a Simone Weil or a Chet Raymo.[11] And it's been literature's loss.

ᖽᐸ

BUT ALL is not lost. By showing John of the Cross's unlikely path to spiritual perfection, we get a first *variety*, albeit medieval, of the lengths one God-infused enthusiast will go. Such audacity haunts nonfiction testaments: confession, autobiography, devotion, essay, memoir. These brachial forms let us see the winding, uneven expanse of the territory we're heading into, terrain I and others measure much as Lewis and Clark mapped the Louisiana Purchase while they trekked. The continental size also mirrors the time of its long, slow coming into being. Across two millennia, writers have enlarged their connection to holy texts and aerie ideals with greater confidence in their own transcendentally puzzling experience. Mindful of the gradual change and its delta-like spread, I find that writers who are marked by liminal adventure fall into two neighboring topographies, basin and range.

One (the range) is the lyric. Poem, prayer, song, hymn, and such select Bible verses as the beatitudes and the psalms. These forms mimic the transcendent by marrying the metaphor and the metaphysical in language. In England, celestial queries are exquisitely rendered in John Dryden's Christian humanist verse, in William Blake's *Songs of Innocence and of Experience*, in Gerard Manley Hopkins's sprung-rhythm poems on God's grandeur. Down the bookish eras, poets pinnacle heaven as their keenest wish, endowing paradise with a euphoria our species can never (again) reach. Such versifiers compact the sublime into stanzaic space with pithy shots of spiritual adrenaline.

The other (the basin) is the discursive narrative—one that proceeds via an often-unwieldy mix of argument, testament, commentary, a tone pensive if not grave, and an anecdote-rife, partial or full life story. In this form, the roomier extensions of life-writing allow tellers to intermingle the epiphanic and the summational. The result may bear some relationship to the faith-forged confession but is, in the hands of today's eclectic masters, a differently imagined voyage of experiential wonder. These books dominate the current practice, on which, in coming chapters, I will focus.

Among the principal testaments of faith in English is Daniel Defoe's *Robinson Crusoe* (1719). The book has been described as a spiritual autobiography, an epic travelogue, an epistolary confession, and the first novel in English. This hero's journey captures the risk-taking exploit for which Englishmen of the eighteenth century longed. Call it the adventure of the colonial entrepreneur—who is also a slaver, an imperialist, a barbarous pilgrim, not to mention a cannibal tamer and killer—saddled with Christian righteousness. (Crusoe, who is shipwrecked oceans away from London's Great Plague, stows one book: the Bible.) The character's voice, its tone high-mindedly penitent, speaks to what David Lyle Jeffrey calls "the protagonist's experience . . . from original sin and alienation through exile, wandering, and providential intervention to a discovery and reading of the Bible, which then interprets life retrospectively, bringing about repentance, conversion, and rescue."[12]

Defoe's classic is, Jeffrey notes further, "the progenitor of the modern novel," realistic fiction, a lie or exaggeration that tells the truth. In the uphill struggle of much spiritual narrative, whose authors create physical and moral trials they must pass, a form eventually crystallizes.

This form—which we now call the spiritual memoir—features a compelling narrative, often to an exotically new place, where a man or woman who lives by his or her wits and under the veiled grace or outright absence of God is challenged, transformed, and, on occasion, redeemed. Such works blend the "I" of the writer and his creation, the "I" of the narrator. Such works posit alternatives to, or argue with, the precepts of the author's religion, if he or she has or has lost one. Such works unscroll a death-defying plot, perspire with detail, foreshadow harrowing events, and, when necessary, load and lengthen and hold onto their mountaintop moments of spiritual liberation with awe.

But before *all that* complication, there's a middle way, which need not shepherd one's higher love down the sticky sidewalk of one's quotidian survival, which need not tally three hundred pages and years of intemperate searching. It's a compromise between basin and range, between lyric and discursive—the spiritual essay.

NOTES

1. Thomas Merton: *Spiritual Master; The Essential Writings*, ed. Lawrence Cunningham (New York: Paulist Press, 1992), 15.

2. Some readers will recognize my paraphrase of what may be the most precise of all quotations about the writer's craft: "A writer is not so much someone who has something to say as he is someone who has found a process that will bring about new things he would not have thought of if he had not started to say them." William Stafford, *Writing the Australian Crawl: Views on the Writer's Vocation* (Ann Arbor: University of Michigan Press, 1978), 17.

3. Eric A. Havelock, *The Muse Learns to Write: Reflections on Orality and Literacy from Antiquity to the Present* (New Haven: Yale University Press, 1986).

4. Erasmus (ca. 1466–1536) translated this sentence differently: "In the beginning was the Speech." The idea is that God spoke the Word long before his followers discovered *writing,* and then wrote his Word down. Speech lacks the carved-into-stone solidity that Text has. It is inescapable that so-called holy texts (aka speech acts) of Christianity and Judaism *happen* before writing, and yet the writing lays the groundwork for the religion's truth claims. For my purposes, this means our interpretation of religious/spiritual writing is based more on the rhetoric of literature and less on the rhetoric of speech.

5. I am not including such post-Augustine philosopher-theologians as Peter Abelard, Thomas Aquinas, Meister Eckhart, Søren Kierkegaard, and others, in part because the vast majority of Christian authors, including these, are theological writers. Very few chew the grit of personal narrative; they don't sink into the personal as witness, having so few models, Augustine notwithstanding. At the same time, I acknowledge the importance of sacred-like textual and artistic monuments such as those to the "American faith." These we might call, expanding the community, secular scripture: the United States Constitution and the Bill of Rights; films like *It's a Wonderful Life* and *Taxi Driver*; paintings like *Nighthawks* and *Freedom from Want*; and books like *Adventures of Huckleberry Finn, To Kill a Mockingbird,*

True Grit, and *Uncle Tom's Cabin,* of which Harriet Beecher Stowe remarked, "I did not write it. God wrote it. I merely did His dictation."

6. St. John of the Cross, *Dark Night of the Soul,* trans. Mirabai Starr (New York: Riverhead Books, 2002). You'll need some backbone to read the secondhand accounts of his brutal Inquisition-blessed confinement. He was often starved and regularly lashed by the Spanish Catholic authorities. Starr labels him "Spain's favorite poet and most confusing theologian" (xvii).

7. I suspect this is as good a spot as any to distinguish soul and spirit, words that seem interchangeable but which are not. In *Webster's New Dictionary of Synonyms* (Springfield, MA: Merriam-Webster, 1984), soul "usually suggests a relation to or a connection with a body or with a physical or material entity to which it gives life or power." Thus the familiar verse in Matthew: "Thou shalt love the Lord thy God with all thy heart, and with all thy soul, and with all thy mind" (22:37). Or Mark 8:36: "For what does it profit a man to gain the whole world and lose his soul." Soul is like a taproot of our species, as in "it often takes a war to lay bare the *soul* of a people." We hunt high and low for our soulmates. We recognize from 1776 Thomas Paine's "times that try men's souls." African Americans rally around soul music and soul power, *The Souls of Black Folk* and *Soul on Ice.* Countless other examples are available.

In my first few pages, I described spirit as a temperamental force. *Webster's Synonyms* notes further that spirit "suggests an opposition or even an antithesis to what is physical, corporeal, or material and often a repugnance to the latter." The poor may be "blessed in spirit" despite their poverty. Native Americans honor the Great Spirit, which connotes a kind of moral magnetism found in the Earth and from which civilized peoples stray. Even as the body wears out, the spirit survives. The spirit models itself, again from *Webster's,* as "signs of excellent physical, or sometimes, mental, health as ardor, animation, energy, and enthusiasm."

Angels and devils have no souls; it's their spirits that do the haunting. I like this ambiguity: Spirit requires a body or a soul through which its immateriality, paradoxically, is experienced. When we "obey the *spirit* rather than the letter of a law," we move beyond a prescribed action. We measure intent, apply moral leniency, and decide cases individually. Spirit is slippery and inchoate when it's roaming, single-minded and leading the way when it's lit.

Soul feels permanent, spirit evasive; one clothed, the other unclad. The soul is immortal. F. Scott Fitzgerald writes to try and discover the "American soul." Joyce forges the "uncreated conscience of his race" in the "smithy of his soul."

Spirit comes close to immortality as well. But it is often more func-tional, giving us vitalism, our sanguine natures, exalted emotions, and an alchemical ability to reconstitute the self or any other object it chooses to inhabit.

8. *The Cloud of Unknowing*, trans. Carmen Acevedo Butcher (Boston: Shambhala Books, 2009), a manuscript from the late fourteenth century by an unknown author, states that God "can be loved but not thought. By love God can be embraced and held, but not by thinking" (21). A mystic from earlier in the same century, Richard Rolle, asks what is God: "I say that thou shalt never find an answer to this question. I have not known; angels know not; archangels have not heard. Wherefore how wouldest thou know what is unknown and also unteachable?" *The Fire of Love,* trans. Richard Misyn, in *Richard Rolle Collection* (London: Aeterna Press, 2015), 56.

Scribes and scholars, however, then and now, declare that via writ-ing and speech God *is* knowable because he has communicated his being partly *in* words, which are further sanctified by their inerrancy. Thus, there shouldn't be much doubt that what he says he is *in language*, he is. Or do we just disregard this in favor of his "working in mysterious ways"? This liter-ate and literary aspect of God's being is, for me, central to the necessity of religious and spiritual discourse. To discuss, debate, believe, and disbelieve such being. To argue that language can't render it is a copout.

9. T. Corbishley and J. E. Biechler, "Mysticism," in *The New Catholic Encyclopedia*, 2nd ed. (Farmington, MI: Gale Group, 2003), 10:113.

10. Carol Harrison, "The Rhetoric of Scripture and Preaching," in *Augustine and His Critics* (New York: Routledge, 2002), 223.

11. Were the science essaying of Raymo's books better known! For example, *Honey from Stone: A Naturalist's Search for God* (1987) plumbs the physicist's year spent communing with nature on a peninsula, geologically and ornithologically alive, in western Ireland: "If I am to encounter God, it must be as the ground for 'things seen.' If I am to encounter mystery, it must be within the interstices of 'things known'" (112).

12. *Oxford Guide to Ideas and Issues in the Bible* (New York: Oxford University Press, 2002), 296–97.

The Spiritual Essayist

The purpose of art is to lay bare the questions
hidden by the answers.

—*James Baldwin*

The spiritual essay anchors the biggest part of the briefest
moment, an economy of insight, if you will, that the long-
winded autobiography and memoir do not share. This economy
allows writers to impress upon us that they have grasped the
spirit's light even though it has already flashed by. In addition,
its brevity engenders flexibility: the essay can turn on a dime,
go against itself, and come back or keep roaming. The essayists
I discuss—D. H. Lawrence, Langston Hughes, Bruce Lawrie—
succeed in their abstract/sensual marriage by remaining lyri-
cally intimate as much as numinously alert, dwelling loosely but
fixedly on the form's brevity, compaction, and intensity. These
writers must try and angle the profound into the passing of the
profound—no easy task.

Among the finest spiritual essays in English is Lawrence's
"The Spinner and the Monks."[1] In 1912, the writer and Frieda

von Richthofen, having fallen lust-mad for each other, spent the winter/spring seasons on Lake Garda in Gargnano, Italy. High above Gargnano and its tangled streets sits the church of San Tommaso. The small chapel, which Lawrence espies from the lakefront, seems to float in the sky, pondering, like the author, the snow-capped peaks of the Tyrol. Climbing cobblestone streets up through the village, passing walled houses atop steep stairways, he discovers San Tommaso's terrace, "suspended . . . like the lowest step of heaven" (21), a place with an earthen sacredness in between (or joining) sky and Earth. He enters the sanctuary and inhales "a thick, fierce darkness of the senses" (22). His soul shrinks, he says, and he hurries outside.

There, in the courtyard, he finds an old woman spinning. More strangeness. "She made me feel as if I were not in existence" (22). Still, there's something in her he desires, something in her he fears. It's unclear. Speaking with her in his poor Italian, he shapes their encounter by painting concrete detail like Renaissance portraiture. "Her eyes were clear as the sky, blue, empyrean, transcendent. They were clear, but they had no looking in them. Her face was a sun-worn stone" (23). Lawrence, the vagabond Englishman who can "read" a people's soul (Italians are "Children of the Shadow"), compares the woman to "the visible heavens, unthinking." She is "without consciousness of self," a state that nettles Lawrence, a man whose senses are easily aggrandized. This peasant is "not aware that there was anything in the universe except *her* universe" (24).

In his description, Lawrence moves the old woman from a servile condition to an archetype—a glowing personification of the unconscious. An otherness. Like the stars. He places the woman, metaphorically, into the firmament, where his being, momentarily, is absorbed into the "macrocosm," the universe that she represents. But, he declares, "the macrocosm is not me." He is the microcosm. So, he concludes, "there is something which is unknown to me and which nevertheless exists." The woman's bearing lets Lawrence address the void-like divide between him and the nonhuman. He's stunned: "There is that which is not me," he writes, over and again, as if this were a newly discovered substance like a spaceship or an artificial heart (24).

He walks on, going higher, picking primroses, lamenting the waning sun. He stops to gaze down into a garden, full of "bony vines and olive trees" (28). There two monks are walking and talking, in late afternoon light, unseen by him. Here is yet another rapprochement between Lawrence and the mystical, the "not me," a scene in which "it was as if I were attending with my dark soul to [the monks'] inaudible undertone" (29). They are walking "backwards and forwards," a phrase he repeats several times; they are busy striving, in tandem, pacing and turning back to pace and turn again. This "backwards and forwards" between life and death, now and then, soul and matter, is like a fulcrum. "Neither the blood nor the spirit spoke in them," Lawrence writes, "only the law, the abstraction of the average" (30). The monks embody a kind of neutrality: being *in* the world yet also passing *through* it, which Lawrence broods upon as his, as our lot, while the old woman is existence itself, its psychic wholeness, observable but unembraceable, which Lawrence yearns to possess. Still, he dreads this come-and-gone sensation. Why? Such flight defuses his nature, which pushes him to capture and hold, for a time, the capricious realm he pursues. Indeed, his prose, too, walks "backwards and forwards," contemplating existence and evanescence, carrying water, chopping wood, before and after this hilltop moment. It is as discoverable as it is unknown.

Then a "meeting-point" arrives, and Lawrence takes "possession of the unknown" with a salty question: "Where in mankind is the ecstasy of light and dark together, the supreme transcendence of the afterglow, day hovering in the embrace of the coming night like two angels embracing in the heavens . . . ?" (31). Where is it? It is there, right in front of him, he realizes. But it is also equally *unrealized*, its elusiveness its reality. *Where* is also where Lawrence sees what "is not me," that is, the apprehending consciousness with which he accepts, satisfied, *his* ultimate absence.

Thus, the final paragraph.

> Where is the supreme ecstasy in mankind, which makes
> day a delight and night a delight, purpose an ecstasy and
> a concourse in ecstasy, and single abandon of the single
> body and soul also an ecstasy under the moon? Where is
> the transcendent knowledge in our hearts, uniting sun and
> darkness, day and night, spirit and senses? Why do we not
> know that the two in consummation are one; that each is
> only part; partial and alone for ever; but that the two in
> consummation are perfect, beyond the range of loneliness
> or solitude? (31)

The spinner and the monks in their Italianate bowers trig-
ger in Lawrence one of life's knottiest queries: Why can't we
see that the supposed opposition of body and soul is nothing of
the kind, that they are not severed but whole? We can't see this
because, as Lawrence shows us, we are the agents of that severing—the me and the not me. In his climb, he passes a clothmaker
and robed walkers, and he is empowered by them to categorize
and name and psychologize and represent and even praise their
otherness. He lingers on them long enough so he will, eventually,
see their difference or, better, his inability to merge with them.
Beautifully, he *essays*: feels the season, observes its flowers, daw-
dles with its companions. And yet, ultimately, his ending is full of
passionate irony. I mark his words: *Why do we not know?* Indeed,
nothing stops him or us from coming and going, "backwards and
forwards," our bobbins spinning us into yarn and wool. In short,
this is the spiritualized tension Lawrence is famous for, a man who
lingers with the "bony vines and olive trees," who conjures the
ashen "not knowing," who rises with the "cloudy knowing." All
that to-and-fro—a delight for this reader—to be reminded of
Lawrence's *what is not me.*

As with nearly all of Lawrence, there's a lesson to heed: if
you wish to lay bare the spiritual questions, disinterred from their

religious answers, let the writing indulge the body and its felt abstractions, and the spirit will speak.

🙠

A SECOND spiritual contender is Langston Hughes's widely beloved tale "Salvation," from his autobiography, *The Big Sea* (1940).[2] Hughes tells us that "going on thirteen," he, young Langston, was saved from sin—saved, "but not really" (18). At a children's session in the church, where he and other kids would "see and hear and feel Jesus in your soul" (19), Langston waits while the minister asks the "little lambs" to come forward. A few hesitate, but most go to the altar. And there, by their voluntary presence, they are saved. Except Langston and another boy, Westley. Neither budges; Langston is not feeling it. But it's hot, and the hymns keep insinuating, and the preacher keeps intoning, and the flock keeps expecting, until Westley finally capitulates: "God damn! I'm tired o' sitting here. Let's get up and be saved," he says to Langston, and so Westley goes to the front of the church. And he is saved. Now, from every corner, the hanky-waving faithful and Langston's family besiege him, the last straggler, to get up. They pray for him "in a mighty wail of moans and voices." And, though he feels he wants to receive the Lord, nothing happens. He waits again. But still he can't see Jesus. Seeing Westley, happily swinging his legs up front, Langston muses, "God had not struck Westley dead for taking his name in vain or for lying in the temple" (20).

So. At last Langston gets up and saunters to the front of the church. And he is saved. Voilà! Lord and congregation propitiated. The dominoes have fallen.

That night, however, after the hurrahs of the family have settled and Langston is alone in bed, he cries. His aunt hears him and comes into his room. His tears, she says, are the Holy Ghost reminding him that he has seen Jesus. The everlasting has arrived in his life for good. But no, Langston thinks, his tears are his shame for lying: "I couldn't bear to tell her," he writes, "that I had lied, that I had deceived everybody in the church, that I hadn't seen

Jesus, and that now I didn't believe there was a Jesus any more, since he didn't come to help me" (21).

How simply wrought yet religiously portentous this confession is. Several things are true. The initiation passed, the emotional purge exacted, Langston is saved in the eyes of the church members; he is saved by his conscience, the opposite of what his family treasures him for receiving; and he is saved by the querulous surprise of his self-disclosure. He knows that what they believe and what he believes—which each would swear to—are the same as they are different. Salvation and faked salvation—river and bank, sun and moon. Doesn't this happen often whenever we are tapped by the rank-and-file to bow our heads in prayer for the dearly departed or to stand for the seventh-inning rendition of "God Bless America"? How many of us, caps in hand, embarrassed faces, dodgy hearts, relish little of what we're supposed to and, instead, feel that the land-that-I-love or the deity-on-high fervor is a public face we're preternaturally unable to feign. The degree to which we hide an absent belief is also the degree to which we hope such an absence might be acknowledged.

The story begins with church members meandering through the sleepy hymn "The Ninety and Nine." Despite the tune's avowal that the lone stray sheep (young Langston), brought back to the fold, is the most blessed of the flock, another counter-certainty raises its head: there is, for young Langston, no God except the God who isn't there, a strangely satisfying hollow that awakens the writer's conscience. Reverse salvation—that which is presumed to ground his life, the weight of the Old Rugged Cross, he discovers he has no desire to lug. But that's not the point. The point is, how does he, how do we live with ourselves if we protect others from knowing what we genuinely feel?

It is not odd that the writer admits his strength as a failure: that's part of the confessional tradition. But it is odd to have learned a kind of doublespeak that shielded those good gospel women who raised and loved him from his disbelief, women to whom he could only disclose, while young, his apostate identity except *in the guise of* telling the truth—showing he was saved when he wasn't and wouldn't be.

✌

HUGHES'S SPIRITUAL pivot comes from an artist whose sensibility our culture has deftly fitted him with. To live loyally, to be indoctrinated into a religious community, is the lot of the child whose "participation" is typically no more than an accident of birth. In charismatic or Baptist-style congregations (compare James Baldwin's *Go Tell It on the Mountain*) reside the public means to—and a performance of—salvation. You are how you conform to your church; you are *not* how the church conforms to you. But despite this tilt, Hughes upholds his individuality, if stealthily and deceptively, within the community, which is the lot of the adult observer, the later-assessing writer.

For Hughes, such hiding in plain sight, enduring ambiguity, is best suited to the internal personal drama of the tale. There, the reader is prodded to interpret motives and decisions without the author's interference, though sometimes such authorial guidance does appear. There, the writer avoids—*should* avoid—the overt preaching or teaching rhetoric of religious tracts and devotional formulae.

In a word, Hughes's spirituality is his character. The conflicting motives are remarkable. Consider, first, that Jesus got Langston to go to the front of the church; consider, second, that Langston went up there of his own free will because, Jesus having failed to nudge him and the church demanding he conform, he strolled up on his own. The first posits a truth that wisely directs our behavior from the outside, though it's also thought of as an inner push or conscience; the second posits that the source is enigmatic at best because it can be contrived or, in certain people, managed because painful consequences come to those who mess with the sanctimony others, chiefly members of one's family, hold dear. That Hughes conveys the subtlety of both with such a simple narrative is, as I say, uncanny.

What's more, he conveys an even stronger ambiguity, which I call flawed reliability. No story is wholly good or bad, so the deconstructionists have taught us, and no author can be wholly credible. All confession is, in part, unreliable. In fiction and nonfiction,[3] modern writers build characters with stark fallibility if they wish readers to trust their creations as sharing our culture's doubt and delusion. A character—think Humbert Humbert, testifying at his trial, in Lolita—has to engage with his reliability *as his story*. With "Salvation," the fallibility of young Langston's conviction is everywhere present in the story. The piece discloses the constant skirmish he has with church rules. His family and Westley, in particular, do not see what we do: that going up front is a success and a failure.

And there's something even bigger. Trust. The reader's trust. I trust Hughes because he seems to say that an individual's salvation cannot be known by other people and, in like manner, requires some of that unknowingness *from the author*. In other words, it's easy to fake salvation for a crowd of born-agains, but it's even *easier* to fake it for oneself. I trust those who show me how fallible the teller of the tale might be. How can anyone know—leaving aside gospel women and preachers and the public spectacle of testifying—whether one is saved? How does coming to the front of the church during the high drama of an evangelical threshing salvationally guarantee that when you die the pearly gates will open? You will be saved in the moment as, apparently, all the little lambs that day were "saved," even the tricksters, Westley and Langston. But the question-inviting and begging of such theater is the legacy.

Anyone can conjure the "evidence" of things unseen—ghosts and spirits and highways to heaven. But when writers develop their narrator's psychology, they present competing evidence as well. While things are unseen, they are also seen *for* their unseenness, if you will, *for* their unreliability. Indeed, Hughes defers to the complicated knowingness of the child. Just as the church community tricks children into public testament—heed the call and let the Lord in—the child, in his honesty, divulges where the rabbit is hidden. Saying that makes him a reliable witness to the deception.

(Deconstruction is not easy.)

The child, Langston, is saved by the truth that he wasn't saved. He lies to himself and then refuses to tell the lie to his family until many years later, nearing forty, when he finally opens and owns up in *The Big Sea*. There, the family, if they've read the story, may have learned that faith is not merely a matter of raw belief. It is a matter of tenacious conscience. We like to think that publicly witnessed religious conviction is *by nature* preferable to privately witnessed disbelief. Don't be misled, Hughes argues. If the faith is in anything, it is in the child's instinctual ability to handle paradox and, with it so handled, be at peace with it.

BOTH LAWRENCE and Hughes maximize the literary impact of their evanescent moments. Publishing one hundred years and sixty years ago, the two essayists capture a spiritual sensibility, which, once we examine it, bears the hallmark of today's authors, the individual opposing, if not thwarting, the institutional. By the time we get to the contemporary essay, a resurgent form, we have a growing number of personal collections and scholarly volumes, perhaps the most well-known of the last two decades, the Penguin Books series The Best Spiritual Writing (1998–2013), edited by Philip Zaleski.

Each year, Zaleski assigns an editor to introduce his or her selections. In an early article about the series, he writes that the twenty or so pieces in each compilation consist of "poetry or prose that deals with the bedrock of human existence—why we are here, where we are going, and how we can comport ourselves with dignity along the way." He goes on: spiritual literature engages that "elusive realm . . . where we encounter the great mysteries of good and evil, suffering and death, God and salvation."[4]

The range of each collection, at times, bewilders and disappoints: most collections carry scholarly articles (exegeses on the Koran; an archeological sojourn through Jerusalem) and (one too many) poems that mention Christ or the Father or spirituality, in text or title, and taste overcooked in their own obscurity. It's tough to find veins of gold in Zaleski's mine. This is so, in part, because the lion's share of religious writing is didactic—telling over showing, begetting over persuasion, credal imperative over inner motivation.[5] To his credit, Zaleski agrees: "For every example of good spiritual literature published last year [1998], there were a baker's dozen that embarrassed with promises of instant enlightenment, or explanations of how meditation can make you rich, or revelations of what Jesus really, really said."

In his introduction to *The Best Spiritual Writing, 2011*, the poet Billy Collins recounts his adolescent's religion and its institutional intractability. He details his stint with the Catholics and rails against two of their infuriating maxims: "To be born with original sin seemed flatly unfair; and the claim of the Church to hold the only means of its erasure—baptism—struck me as monopolistic" (xv). During college, Collins drifted into unbelief, via "utterly seductive" writers like Wordsworth and Dickinson, Beckett and Jack Kerouac (the Beats' name comes from *beatific*: desolation angels and seraphic outcasts). He was also lured into theological debate, in which several Ferrari-sharp minds try to prove, logically, God's existence.

Exploring his existential dilemmas via poetry, Collins says, in his introduction, that the numinous arrives only in "veil-dropping moments of insight" (xxi). "For the majority of its followers, religion is less of an experience than it is a set of beliefs, a moral code, and a picture of the hereafter. But spiritual experience . . . is indeed an *experience*, usually marked by a sense of sudden entry into another dimension. This spiritual life is one of surprising glimpses, which often resist verbal description, as distinct from a sustained set of theological beliefs and doctrines, which can be explained to anyone, as any proselytizer knows" (xxiii).

If these insights "resist" the verbal, as Collins argues, why write about it at all? Why not just sing anthems or recite the Lord's Prayer as legions do? First, such practices by artists or by

mass assent do not exclude each other: transcendentalists like
Thoreau stayed away from church, while Emerson adored the
pastor's perch. Second, the surprising glimpse *resists* the verbal;
it neither stops nor forbids inquiry. Writing to occupy the Holy
Spirit found zealotry in the four gospel authors, in Paul, in Augustine, in the medieval visionaries Hildegard von Bingen and
Richard Rolle—all sought God's grace by taking up their pens.
Third, Collins's worry, that spiritual intuition and poetic ver-
ity are antagonistic, reaffirms the necessity of metaphor, which
pushes one "to turn toward other terms" when translating the ineffable. Such descriptive fury ignites John Donne's Holy Sonnets.
God is a lustful tart, whom one poem's narrator accuses: "You
ravish me." In kind, God makes the narrator think his hunger to
be loved should be validated by pain: "Batter my heart," "bend /
Your force to break, blow, burn, and make me new." The believer
is prey, his faith the fate of a prisoner. Locked up, he "wisheth
himselfe delivered from prison." But hauled from his cell by the
hangman, he "wisheth that still he might be imprisoned" and
escape the terror of execution and God's judgment. The associations writers uncover and fertilize are limitless.

DELVING MORE deeply into the Zaleski volumes, I locate at least
one desert bloom: "Who Am I, Lord, That You Should Know My
Name?" by Bruce Lawrie.[6] This three-page piece, published in
Portland in 2009, is among the most indelibly spiritual essays ever
penned. It is directed to the author's "severely mentally retarded"
son Matty and involves Lawrie and a God who, in the writer's
imagination, afflicts the most innocent and promises them heaven
as their reward. Every night when Lawrie puts the boy to bed he
sings him praise songs (the title is a line from one), cherishes their
touch, and hopes the act soothes the boy's condition.

I start singing the next song in our nightly rotation as I
brush his hand against my whiskers, first his palm and then

the back of his hand. He explores my face with his fingertips
and then he covers my mouth gently. I sing into his palm,
imagining the reverberations vibrating down into his little
soul. How does he experience me? What am I in his world?
I don't know. I may never know. (114)

The essay's final paragraph (of ten) is a wish for Matty's coming
life in heaven. Lawrie whispers to the boy that his ordeal will end:
"Soon, Matty. Soon." Before this dark wish, Lawrie describes the
heaven where Matty has "a healthy body and a lovely wife," a son
of his own, where father and son drink a beer and the author invites
Matty's son, Lawrie's grandson, to "fall asleep in my lap, a sweaty
load of spent boy pinning me to my chair on the deck." But none
of this wipes out Matty's punishing operations, "the straps tying his
hands to the hospital bed rails so he wouldn't pull the needles out,"
a boy clueless "why the people around him had suddenly begun
torturing him" (115). (We never learn his specific "retardation" or
his treatment.)

A brief list of sour apples torments Lawrie. He remembers "all
the other things [Matty's] been robbed of. Meeting a girl. Playing catch. . . . Making love." Matty's heaven is the reverse of this
one—where he will get what most of us *here* already have: roman-
tic love, losing that love, and finding it again. The result is that he,
the father, keeps the hope of better times alive when the boy's pain
will end. As will Lawrie's pain, too. When Matty dies, he'll awaken
healed; his father will be there, too, and, Lawrie writes, "God will
carve out a little slice of eternity for us; our own private do-over."
"Soon, Matty. Soon" (114–15).

Lawrie keeps reporting on and imagining Matty in these con-
trasting states—in the boy's richly intimate but agonizing actual
life and in the dream home his father insists the boy will one day
occupy. His earthly life "comes at him as if blasted from a water
cannon," thick with an "indecipherable roar" and "white noise."
The specifics grind to dust our sense of a child's due. Matty is "unable to walk on his own," is "legally blind in one eye," has endured

"operations," "IVs," "needles," and "countless blood draws," among other pains—according to Lawrie, all these weigh, slab-heavy, on "his little soul." Yet Matty is loved and he "loves"—prizes his routine, "craves" its "repetition," and routinely toddles "off to sleep." Just before that moment, Matty "lets out a sigh that tells me [Lawrie] everything's right in his world" (113).

"He finds the cool sheet safe, slings a skinny leg over the bed, and hauls himself up on top, moving rapidly before the bed can escape. He lies on his back rocking back and forth in bed, body rigid, a crease-eyed smile lighting his face, letting out an ecstatic *aaahh*" (114).

It's a heartbreaking essay, the narrator twisting between realms real and dreamlike. Does Matty feel his father's cherishing him, and yet also sense his dad's craving for him to be a "normal" boy? Does Matty grasp the gap between the human drama and the supernatural fantasy? The human drama is universally felt; the fantasy conjures up a Christian cosmos. Heaven is where all beings are, if not copacetic, then fixed. Heaven, where wishing the boy healthy is granted, where there's a new Matty, the saved or the corrected or the replaced Matty: the deity makes everything right, including movie dates, a first kiss, a first night of passion, arriving unblemished *after* life. But not during.

In the *not during* simmers the hurt. The more another boy is wished for, the more the boy in the bed is unchanged and the more the father despairs. Worse, Lawrie has to balance the affection he has for his boy against the future "version" of Matty he obsesses over. That version of the self which suggests we have no say in the random nature of our punishments, a tune also sung by Job: "For he breaketh me with a tempest, and multiplieth my wounds without cause" (9:17).

That Lawrie has called upon God to give Matty the brain he should have had because—you guessed it—God dealt him the bad hand, the endless surgeries no child should endure, is irrational, if not absurd. Doesn't Matty's condition suggest, at least, in Lawrie's mind, that God will fully heal Matty only when Matty is removed from his dad's care? Why doesn't Lawrie abdicate his conviction once he discovers the petitioned one is the abuser? Or is he? Perhaps Lawrie should, but he doesn't. Giving up on heaven is not in the author's nature, nor in his boy's interest. Besides, what father abandons hope while his child suffers?

None does.

⅊

READING LAWRIE ping-pong between what is and what will be, that is, the *will be* that *should have been,* arouses feelings in me of the darkest hue. Just consider the essay's chafing facts—the boy's torture, the father's piety; the boy's physical burden, the father's sorrow; the boy's velvety prison, the father's holding its bars in place. More disturbing is the chamber opera of false hope. How it must upset Lawrie to stifle the fact that Matty's time on earth has been robbed while he, the father, sings him their bedtime song! To have it boil down to Lawrie wishing the boy dies soon, sooner than the father wants, and loving the boy's pleasures still seems utterly hopeless.

What I find frightening in this almost mockingly Christian Christian essay is that merely acknowledging the boy's suffering *exacts* the death wish. That Lawrie allows it. That he doesn't apologize for it. That he makes fervent his hastening it: "Soon, Matty. Soon." A loving execution.

Such is spiritual? Yes. It arrives, first, in the glimpse, the surprise of Lawrie's executioner's ardor. It is apparently an option, and so off-putting that Lawrie can only state it and turn away. The hope that Lawrie might grant his son's death when God will not I think of as malevolent. But it is also supernal, not unlike petitionary prayer. This death-dream invites a truth about what God won't decide but will defer to us. That truth would have remained submerged had Lawrie not pushed the essay to press the desire of heaven against the ludicrousness of fate. Lawrie presses anyway. The idea is made more profound because it is succinct. The conciseness scares everyone and forces the whole responsibility for the boy's mortality onto Lawrie's shoulders. What's flummoxing is that Lawrie wants what he can't have and can do nothing about what he feels he's steering himself *to do*—hasten the end of Matty's life so Matty might have his heaven.

Pico Iyer writes, in his introduction to *The Best Spiritual Writing, 2010,* "Spirituality . . . arises out of the disjunction between us and the transcendent as much as out of the occasional union; it lies, as in any love affair, in the attempt to draw closer to a reality that we sense inside ourselves (though sometimes, in our uncertainty, we call it only 'possibility'), and in our longing to live in the truth that is self-evident whenever we're where we ought to be" (xiv).

I want to underline "disjunction"—and the longing that occurs because of it. That longing crosses desire with transcendence, what we know is there, what we can't have, yet *we want nonetheless.* Spirituality is a chasm between a beckoning, absent reality and where we are stuck, yearning for that reality. Sometimes a bridge materializes and a union ensues. But, considering human complaints about fate's unfairness, most of the time we are left wishing a union were so.

I note that Lawrie is not angry with God's power in heaven or on earth. In fact, heaven often manifests its palliative spirit during the nighttime ritual joy of father and son at bed. It's only the persistent reminder of "all the other things he's been robbed of" that nettles Lawrie into a quiet rage—a rage, I should note, made more palpable because Lawrie has chosen to evoke that rage. Caveat emptor indeed.

We arrive at a dystopic vision of the supreme being, a negation modern Christian theologians call absurd. That the Maker who made me warts and all wants me fixed only in death. There's no greater conundrum for the undeserved torture of a child. But resolving that wrong, that fate, is not Lawrie's point. The point is to inhabit the trap of longing, which is unresolvable neither by the author nor, this terse tally tells us, by God. Lawrie can only enact the irresolution in prose.

Lawrie digs into this abyss beautifully, sensitively. He exposes his own naïveté about God, examining a childlike hope of heaven whose benevolence is forever delayed. But that who-knows-when—and soon—also justifies such hope, particularly for the father of a disabled son. How compelling to stay with his words, be soaked to the bone on his in-between-ness, which, though wide and deep and wet and frightening, may be the only bardo in which the spiritual lingers, if and when it lingers at all.

WHAT STRIKES me about the Zaleski series—why, I wonder, did it end in 2013 after fifteen years?—is that the volumes isolate, if not magnify, problems with distinguishing religious treatises from spiritual writing and, within the latter, identifying the lyric and the discursive modes, in essay and memoir, respectively, that urge an author to use one mode over another.

That magnification, which the series celebrated, is a good thing; I'm sorry it ended. However, even though I admire Zaleski's desire to categorize the "best spiritual writing," a superlative doesn't mean we know what "spiritual writing" is. Perhaps that's why the series didn't continue—the anthologies did not sell well, "the spiritual essay" need not have a separate venue from the essay, or the literariness of the "form" is hopelessly unstable, its wildly different takes on belief and unbelief (or the hazy combination of the two) rendered *best* inoperative.

Let me probe this another way.

You, the writer, decide to wash the bodies of the dead in New Delhi so you can quit a decade of beer-guzzling and pot-smoking. Or you, the writer, retreat for a summer with real Navajos to real Navajo sweat lodges so you can rediscover your Native American heritage that's been buried for years as a branch manager at Wells Fargo.

How are these essays or stories, short or long, spiritual?

You can hear the goal of each—the desire to move away from a condition where your soul is imprisoned. Or, better, to move toward activities that you suspect are soulful. Which, because of the spiritual connotation, may release that soul. But you probably also hear the danger. It's in assuming searching leads to finding. You can't escape the booze or the bank unless you leave and seek something new. You have to make the break. But what has happened before when you set that goal? Nine times out of ten, failure. This is the trap of trying to sentence yourself to be "more spiritual," assigning yourself outcomes like salvation, redemption, and grace.

I know of no other way around this for the writer than through it. Lawrence's search for the sensual oneness of being, Hughes's search for a way to integrate his disbelief with his church community, and Lawrie's search for a heaven-like, near-time destiny for his son's malady—all come up short as resolution. Where they don't come up short is discovering that writing is far more helpful for the peripatetic soul than we know.

One reason: it is possible that where models of religious security once dominated the tell, today uncertainty calls the shots. A change not in form but in content.

Maybe what matters is that each author takes a swing at the inexplicable. Maybe what matters is that with each at bat we, as readers, glimpse where the inexplicable lies in each author, that death is the end, that there is no answer to evil, that nothing will ever be resolved, that it is as good to know where you're going as it is good to have no idea where you're going. Maybe what matters is simple—that we don't institutionalize the urge to write spiritually as anything other than making the most of that urge.

NOTES

1. D. H. Lawrence, "The Spinner and the Monks," chap. 2 in *Twilight in Italy* (1916), in *D. H. Lawrence and Italy* (New York: Penguin Books, 1972). Essay runners-up from the nineteenth, twentieth, and twenty-first centuries include "Spiritual Laws" and "The Oversoul," by Ralph Waldo Emerson; "The Wind at Djemila" and "Death in the Soul," by Albert Camus; "The Inner Galaxy" and "The Hidden Teacher," by Loren Eiseley; "Fire Watch, July 4, 1952" and "Day of a Stranger," by Thomas Merton;

"The Surgeon as Priest" and "The Exact Location of the Soul," by Richard Selzer; "Let It Go" and "god," by Brian Doyle; "Winter Garden" and "On Intla: Snow That Has Drifted Indoors," by Kathryn Winograd; "Fire Season" and "The Return," by Rick Bass; "God in the Doorway" and "Singing with the Fundamentalists," by Annie Dillard.

2. Langston Hughes, "Salvation," in *The Big Sea* (New York: Hill and Wang, 1993).

3. Speaking briefly of fiction, no American religious or spiritual author can escape the influence of Nathaniel Hawthorne's "Young Goodman Brown" or Flannery O'Connor's "Revelation." O'Connor said that as a Catholic novelist she set herself the narrative challenge to "make belief believable." Add in Baldwin, Mary Gordon, Reynolds Price, Bret Lott, Frederick Buechner, and others who continue the Graham Greene tradition of embodying characters with the novelist's real or imagined religious life crises.

For this book, I have chosen not to include fiction. Such would be too unwieldy and create too great a contrast with the author-altering testimonies of religious and spiritual confession. Besides, religion-based writers are, as I repeat, a dwindling minority, disappearing with most things theological and institutional.

Paul Elie nicely sums up the dearth of Christian themes in literary fiction, post-O'Connor, who died in 1964: "In America today Christianity is highly visible in public life but marginal or of no consequence in a great many individual lives. For the first time in our history it is possible to speak of Christianity matter-of-factly as one religion among many; for the first time, it is possible to leave it out of the conversation altogether." http://www.nytimes.com/2012/12/23/books/review/has-fiction-lost-its-faith.html.

4. "God Help the Spiritual Writer," *New York Times*, January 10, 1999.

5. In my reading, I estimate that 80 percent of the Bible is moralizing and historical tedium (Paul's snap at women to keep their mouths shut in church is indicative of such sermonizing). What to say of the 20 percent? No doubt it's poetic and profound: some of the Psalms; the lines on charity in 1 Corinthians; the book of Job; the stories of Ruth and Rebecca; the occasional equivocation in the Pauline letters; and more. Who can outdo this muscular verse from Isaiah 9:6, which echoes in Handel's *Messiah:* "For unto us a child is born, unto us a son is given: and the government shall be upon his shoulder: and his name shall be called Wonderful, Counsellor, The mighty God, The everlasting Father, The Prince of Peace."

6. Lawrie's essay is reprinted in *The Best Spiritual Writing, 2011.*

The Christian Autobiographer

Both what I know about myself and what I do not
know will therefore be my testimony to you, since
what I know I have seen by your light, and what
I do not know is from my own darknesses, not yet
scattered by your noonday gaze.

—*Augustine*

What does it mean to call religious and spiritual writing
literary? How necessary is this designation? On one hand,
we have the seventeenth-century verse of the metaphysical and devotional poets as well as John Milton, whose headline is Christian
Charity Defeats the Devil. Those authors live in a world biblically
organized, write in a confessional or fabulist voice, and, especially
with Milton's *Paradise Lost,* help fashion a Christian literature
during the English Renaissance. During the eighteenth century,
the majority of Enlightenment writers eschew biblical themes.
They elevate human iniquity and social relations as their primary

concern, and from their efforts a literature, call it secular or humanist, begins to grow. These works eventually undergird a culture's fiercest metanarratives—stories of thwarted freedom: Ahab and the whale, Huck and Miss Watson, Meursault and his indifference.

But the question of literariness remains for one monumental reason—the Bible. The Bible is, indisputably, thought of as the Word of God and, disputably, thought to be a fully flourishing *literary document*.[1] Despite the latter dispute, I realize the autobiography and memoir I'm critiquing owes its themes, tropes, and terminology to the Bible. Indeed, in a book-blessed culture, a religion needs inerrant, testimonial texts whose message is used to convert the wayward. This occurs before a faith-affirming confession is possible. In the Common Era, such books (though few and far between) model a salvaged life, one that is, according to its disciples, rarely achieved. All the more reason to seek it.

Christians believe the Bible is God's word, spoken and transcribed. Its texts include family trees, injunctions, anecdotes, parables, myths, miracles, poetry, and much testimony. Its writers employ syntactic parallelism, synonymous restatement, and naturalistic metaphor. By 1530, the Great Book was given Anglo-Saxon accents and sonorities in William Tyndale's English translation. Eighty years later, his version was further enhanced as the King James Bible. You can hear Tyndale's music in Isaiah 40:8: "The grass withereth, the flower fadeth, but the Word of the Lord shall abide forever."

The Bible regularly uses the word *spirit* (in Greek, *pneuma*): God himself is spirit, as are the ministering angels, the agent by which Mary is impregnated, the inner reward of adhering to divine law, and the gift of kingdom come through Jesus Christ, who bears and dispenses the Holy Spirit. The Holy Spirit descends on Jesus during John's baptism with the metaphor of the descending dove. Spirit manifests through him in his prophecies, his healing arts, and the Sermon on the Mount. To complete the story, Christ has to relinquish his carapaced essence when he dies: "Father, unto your hands I commit my spirit."

In addition to its "holy" label, the word (there are 719 uses of *spirit* in the testaments) carries fatalistic extensions: unless we are hyper-wary, the spirit of evil, already staining flesh, earth, and body, dupes us into desire, vanity, and sin, funneling us, if we're not careful, to perversion, apostasy, and Satan. Here is the foundational contrast. Spirit, in Paul's disseverment, opposes flesh—the former sacred and incorruptible, the latter violable and mundane. Romans 8:6: "For to be carnally minded is death, but to be spiritually minded is life and peace."

Spirit is that which is sent to act on those the man behind the curtain has deemed worthy. One such is Ezekiel (37:1–14). The Lord sends his servant, Ezekiel, into a valley laden with dry bones. The Lord tells him to prophesy over the skeletons, so they hear the word of God. The bones, with the added importuning of the wind, are animated with human substance: skin, muscle, organs, breath. Suddenly an army springs up, a legion of fighters to retake Israel. All this is produced by "the spirit of the Lord" through Ezekiel—because he did as he was told in a kind of divine, unquestioning rapture. The unseen agent uses Ezekiel as his agent to do his bidding. The allegory is as obvious as it is wondrous.

In the Gospel of John, the Word gets top billing *as* God. In John 6:63, Christ says, "The words that I speak unto you [the disciples], they are spirit, and they are life." They also carry meaning—indeed, meaning that sacralizes language as a metamorphic force. It's the force of metonym and synecdoche: The words spoken by Christ and by God—the Word itself—*stand for* part of or, if you like, the whole of Christ and God.

Paul's writing, which pervades the New Testament, asserts that the Spirit's mission on Earth is Christ's mission; they are the same. Or, better, Christ's life and death materialize the Holy Spirit into its earthly cast. Christ is the historical flesh-and-blood hatching of a transcendent reality—the first and last, the one and only, the lone undead human being. In Romans 1:4—the words are Paul's—Christ is "declared to be the Son of God with power, according to the spirit of holiness, by the resurrection from the dead." That is, Christ, crucified and tomb-fled, is resurrected and returns, unveiling for the disciples his stigmatic hands and missionary message. Christ appears and disappears to his followers *as* spirit.

To the larger point, like the monolith in *2001: A Space Odyssey*, Paul makes of spirit an abstraction, an object of thought. This abstraction—which would have been enacted in the drama, poetry, and music of the preliterate era—resides in Paul's words: to turn Jesus into Christ, to turn a human being into a consciousness, to turn a man's story into a savior's text. Christ is transformed into the Holy Spirit and then transformed into scripture in Christ's day and, so it's avowed, for eternity. Such is Paul's moon landing.

Paul's gift: spirit *comes from a holy or a nonhuman source*. Thus, if the spirit is outside the body and placed into people as a reward for their devotion, then we need a church, an institutional placeholder, a delivery system, to bestow the reward. Christians are called to follow Christ's teachings. Its adherents should accomplish "good works." Given exceptional honesty and deeds, an individual becomes a placeholder of spirit himself. Case in point—the moral anchor of Daniel and Philip Berrigan.

IN PAUL'S thirteen New Testament letters, his pronouncements of the precepts of faith far exceed any personal intuition he divulges about himself as the deliverer of those precepts. A quick overview should clarify what I mean.

When we meet Paul, on the road to Damascus, he is Saul of Tarsus, a Hellenistic Jew and Roman citizen. He has spent his adulthood exterminating apostles of Christ, who are called "Jewish Christians." Suddenly, the murderer Saul has a vision, as bright as it is loud. A voice out of the firmament accuses him: Why are you persecuting us? What have we Jewish Christians done to you? Saul demands: Who is speaking? It is Christ, the voice says, who tells Saul he, Jesus, is the chief victim of Saul's persecution. Before

Saul replies, he is blinded by Jesus, by God, by lightning—it's not clear who or what. He is led to Damascus, where, after he has gone without food and water for three days, his sight is suddenly restored. To Saul the Lord has spoken. Reborn as Paul, he begins declaring in every town, around every communal well, that Jesus Christ is the Son of God.

The supernatural snap on the road is among the greatest anointings in Christendom. In *The Conversion on the Way to Damascus*, Caravaggio imagines Paul thrown from his horse and fallen flat on his back—stunned, as it were, into action. In Acts 9:15–16, Luke says of Paul—quoting God—that he "is a chosen vessel unto me, to bear my name before the Gentiles, and kings, and the children of Israel: For I will shew him how great things he will suffer for my name's sake." Paul is rendered missionary, his *new* vocation sent from above via a sound-and-light show as well as from the bitter elixir of self-loathing.

Most Christians venerate the Gospels and the Pauline writings. But the latter do not narrate the Jesus story as the four Gospel authors do. Rather, the writings are *impersonal*, even as they summon devout and high-strung emotions. They rarely soar with telling details or seat-edge tales of Paul's storied career. They reflect the zeal of his church-building charge: to convert Gentiles. Paul's letters seldom, if ever, disclose the vicissitudes of him as a conflict-beleaguered autobiographer.[2]

Here's a pronominal division critical to autobiography and memoir. With first-person narrative, we have one "I," that of the writer. And we have another "I," that of the narrator the writer has created to represent himself on the page. Many narrators have no self-consciousness. They ignore the writer (or, we might say, the writer ignores his narrator), and they just tell the tale.

Paul fits the bill. A man who hears voices, has seizures, is boastful, and wields a messianic cudgel, he's become God and Christ's "chosen vessel," a ship of letter-writing scripture. He writes about what he's been told to—missionize the lost, baptize the strays, reel in the fleeing souls. He is accommodating because rapture offers him no choice. Here is how he says he's vesseled by Jesus: "I am crucified with Christ: nevertheless, I live; yet not I, but Christ liveth in me: and the life which I now live in the flesh I live by the faith of the Son of God, who loved me, and gave himself for me" (Galatians 2:20). Paul is a receiver, a broadcaster, an aggregator. In 1 Corinthians 9:22, he states, "I am made all things to all men, that I might by all means save some." There's no strutting and fretting on his epistolary stage. Indeed, nowhere does Paul show us how he changed from killer to apostle.

What is missing in Paul is a self who is disclosing his truth. What is missing are the words of a writer in whom his inner turmoil is expressed while he's disclosing that truth. Such a calling, alas, awaits a confessional *artist*, some three hundred years hence. When a writer of proven literary skill portrays the deepest concerns of his narrating "I" alongside those of his own—an author who is thinking and feeling, believing and questioning, conforming and psychologizing—we are in the presence of literature's shaman, a truthteller, whom readers trust. From him, we get a more rounded, more reliable, more honest, more capable, more relatable "I," a savvy, interdependent mix of narrator and writer, than an "I" where all things inner are kept at bay.

If there is an "I" in Paul, that "I" is fetal at best.

And fetal that "I" remains until Augustine, bishop of Hippo, brings the faith's inaugural *written* self to a nascent Christianity.

THE FIRST writer in the West to detail his spiritual journey— to emotionally inhabit that journey with flashes and fanfares of literary genius—is Augustine (354–430 CE), author of *Confessions*, published between 397 and 400.[3] In thirteen books, his autobiography is a dialogue with God. In it, he testifies to what he knows and to what he's been instructed by God he should know. Most important, he dwells on his failure to follow those instructions. He knows things, but his experience often counteracts that knowledge. Augustine limns the struggle between his body (bad)

and his soul (good). Simple. But when I read Augustine, I'm shocked by the certainty with which he declares his lusts have been so immoral and his soul so scarred that there's no doubt he'll lose God's grace, and worse, forgo heaven. Such horrors are neither abstract nor credal. They are real, roiling his body and mind, not to mention the "sin-ridden" lives of everyone. His God seems to have one *writerly* demand: Who among my small but growing Christian mass will admit the sexual pleasure of his sin? Augustine volunteers.

Writing of his shame, Augustine says he's failed to acquire the virtues God commands of him. (Alan Watts: "God did not give us commandments in order that we should obey them, but rather to prove that we could not.")[4] What's more, Augustine recognizes what he *should* do: convert, confess, renounce pagan desires, and receive the Holy Spirit. If he proves worthy—in life and in writing—God heavens him home. Augustine demands this not of God but of himself.

Eventually, the day arrives when what he demands of himself will prove worthy of God.

It is August, 386 CE. Augustine is thirty-two, living in Milan and teaching rhetoric. He is tormented, "soul-sick," and blubbering uncontrollably to a witnessing friend. Why the tears? He's an ADD mix of sex maniac and self-flagellator. He has promised to marry a young girl and is waiting for her to turn twelve, the legal age. In the interim, he continues his depravity with several concubines, hating his weakness. He is enslaved, he writes, in Garry Wills's translation, "My now-ingrained panic was increasing daily, and I daily panted for you" (169–70). At one point, so enamored of his debauchery, he tells God not to save him too soon "from the sick urges I wanted rather intensified than terminated." He moans, "Give me chastity and self-control, but not just yet" (173).

In book 8 of *Confessions*, it is afternoon, and he is crawling into the backyard garden of his home, where he collapses under a fig tree and beseeches God, "How much more" before

his conflict between flesh and spirit ends. He hears a neighboring child say, "Lift! Look!" (181). (Much confusion still exists
about this "voice." Is it Augustine's internal voice? An actual
child, chosen for the sound of his or her innocence? Is it God's
or Christ's voice, echoing Paul's *audition?*) Lift what? The Epistles
of Paul, which are conveniently lying nearby. Augustine does,
and the book falls open to Romans 13:13. He reads the verses
aloud: "Give up indulgence and drunkenness, give up lust and
obscenity, give up strife and rivalries."[5] He is instructed to "clothe
yourself in Jesus Christ the Lord," which for Augustine means to
do away with his beloved "concupiscence," or lusts. He ends the
paragraph with perhaps the greatest reported moment of spiritual
awakening (some might call it the greatest non sequitur) in confessional narrative: "The very instant I finished that sentence,
light was flooding my heart with assurance, and all my shadowy
reluctance evanesced" (182).

Augustine is converted. Or, as Garry Wills makes clear—in
one of his companion books, *Saint Augustine's Conversion* (2004)—
the already Christ-centered Augustine (son of a pagan father and
a nunnish mother) is released from his lust. (Such liberation from
sexual cravings is often construed as "religious freedom," that is,
one is "set free." As in, *Christ, free me from the grip of porn!*)

In any event, voilà, Augustine will—this time for sure—become
celibate.

What? I don't believe him? Yes and no.

In book 8's first half, Augustine, a master of persuasive arguments, outlines seven conversion stories of other pilgrims. He is
telling us that these lost souls were initiated into the faith and,
dear reader, my initiation is coming as well. As stylistic addi-
tives, he quotes Bible verses to stiffen his scholarly backbone for
his pending deliverance. An example: "So by experiment upon
myself I was coming to realize what I had read of how 'the desire of the flesh opposes the spirit, the desire of the spirit opposes
the flesh,' for I was experiencing both—yet I felt more identified
with that in me which I now wanted than with that in me that I

found wanting" (168). In quoting Galatians 5:17, he not only uses God's cleverly juxtaposed antithesis to evidence his core conflict but, more strongly, owns the change in himself by emphasizing the sentence-closing arrangement of his own juxtaposition: *which I now wanted* vs. *that I found wanting.*

As book 8 develops and he punches up the drama of his surrender, Augustine advances his personal case. He takes pains to purify his sin and self by writing a public document, which is also a private affirmation of the Christian journey, designed to last as text—printed, inalterable. The point is to insure his salvation *through testimony.* But such testimony wasn't just for the few; the dream was much, much bigger. To convince those in power, educated in Greek and Latin, Augustine, one of the era's great rhetoricians, sewed his talent into the fabric of the new creed. Even though only a small portion of the *free* population was literate, it makes sense that the writerly form he invented and passionately practiced reflected well on his class. Once the 1 percent were on board, they spread the good news to the masses, who dutifully followed, though it took centuries to translate Scripture into common tongues and teach those tongues how to read.

How exactly does Augustine textualize salvation? He discovers that if he moves from the rhetoric of persuasion by means of analysis and logic—commonly grasped by the educated class—to the rhetoric of persuasion by means of story and emotion—commonly grasped by the everyday sinner—he has his doubly bewitching form. Indeed, the educated can *point* the masses to Augustine as their and everyone's model.

Here, then, it gets interesting. Some argue that Augustine's conversion happens *to* him, is visited upon him like a spell, and only when he's at the end of his rope. (Apropos is the line from Leonard Cohen's "Suzanne": "Only drowning men could see him.") But the compositional structure of *Confessions* belies this idea. At the climax of book 8, Augustine issues a last-ditch admission, in one paragraph (quoted below), of the thwarted turmoil enthralling him, something new to literature—a composed lingering on his confusion and uncertainty at the pinnacle moment when he's being altered, as much by the divine as by *the drama of the prose itself.*

> So sick was I, so tortured, as I reviled myself more bitterly than ever, churning and chafing in my chains, not broken free of them entirely, held more loosely now, but still held, as you were working in my hidden places, with your fierce pity wielding the double whip of fear and shame to prevent my relapse, to prevent the loosening and light bond that still held me from renewing its grip, to grapple me again more tightly than before. My inner self was urging me: Make it now! Make it now! With those words I was moving to a resolution, I was almost there—but was not there. Still, I did not slide all the way back, but braced myself nearby, catching my breath then, renewing the effort, I almost made it—almost—but did not; I was all but touching, all but clasping—but no, I was not there, not yet touching, not yet clasping, not ready to die to death and live to life, still held by the ingrained evil in me over the untrained good in me. The moment when I would become someone different, the closer it came, the terror it struck in me—a terror, however, that no longer wrenched me back or fended me off, but left me hanging. (179)

❧

IN SAINT *Augustine's Conversion,* Garry Wills remarks that in the first sentence of section 25 (quoted above) the author's "grammar tosses about in this long, loosely constructed, and entrammeling [entangled] sentence. A good case of moral quandary *reenacted* in language" (92). Indeed. In my reading, the *reenacted* is the *enacted!* Make it now! Make it now!

If there's a more perfect paragraph than section 25, which initiates the spiritual writer into Western literature, I don't know it. For multiple reasons. First, Wills's *entrammeling:* To entangle, to be so entangled that the entanglement takes over, binds words to emotions. When Augustine writes, "I was almost there—but was not there" and was "more loosely held, but still held" in his chains, I find him nailing himself to the paradox so we feel the full force of its irresolution. Next, the writing is not Bible-laced; the nagging referrals to that book stop. The words are Augustine's. How to tell? The direct address to "you," that is, God, is personal, "you" exercising your will on me. The "you" also bewitches, as Wills shows, in that first entrammeled sentence. Subsequently, the "you" is overtaken, simplified, even controlled by "I." "I" is used nine times. And, with "me" and "my," the personal pronouns proliferate, as if he's stocking up. The emphasis is strategic. We presume this moment of thrashing about happened to Augustine *in the past*, but we also presume that it's happening to him *in his writerly present* and in the present *of our reading*.

I call such testimony *felt* writing.

In addition, the sentences' subjects and objects are the self, different and less impactful from the typical injunctions Augustine resorts to elsewhere, for example, when he writes, "Lord . . . how you liberated me from the chains of carnal yearning tight wrapped around me, and from the drudgery of my secular career" (169). Somehow *carnal yearning* is the not the same as *I was all but touching, all but clasping*. Augustine is trying to inhabit the prose with the immediate rawness of the moment while fast-inking his quill. He's downplaying the theological order of his life and, albeit temporarily, occupying the breath of his deliverance—so we fathom his dilemma.

Augustine wakes up in the paragraph once he realizes he is testifying. He asserts himself via repetition, anchoring and varying the emotion as well as packing a kind of bodily fierceness into the verbs: churn, chafe, grip, grapple, brace, wrench, fend, hang, catch, renew, clasp, touch, ingrain, and untrain, plus the adverbs, loosely and tightly, and the refrain, almost, not yet, almost. He *activates*, indeed *overactivates*, these verbal constructs. He quickens the pulse of the clauses, so they feel twitchy, turning him this way and that.

So brazen is his rhetoric, it's as though he were lifting the rattle-snakes above his head and pure faith was shielding him from their tongues.

As much as I admire the analysis of Marjorie O'Rourke Boyle, she overstates the missionary fervor of Augustine's "divine praises" and misses the "human pleasures" of his self-persecution. She says he preaches too much (true) and emphasizes revelation over rhetoric or personal narrative (not true). She calls his work "an apologetics of pabulum." The word means that which nourishes the soul but is also a diet of bland, insipid, and simplistic words. *Confessions*, she continues, "set the style for the clerical resort to rhetoric as a sop to the laity. With intellectualist bias, Augustine reduced Scripture, already lamented as crude, to divine baby talk" (667).[6]

For me, the genuine Augustine comes in the "baby talk" where the shamed child occupies the emotion so entirely that I get the flawed and fearful author, a penitent and puerile solipsist. I love Michael Higgins's characterization of Augustine's prose: "the inflated language of failed yearning."[7] Augustine's use of the "I" to report on his inner being captures the drama of the man because only he knows how troubled he is. Augustine is our first first-person genius. He originated the self-fabricating "I" as a truthful "I" in literature. For that alone, we study him. And, after such study, I say, it's seldom that much about God; it's quite a lot about Augustine.

Other sections of high personal drama in book 8 include 16–18 and 21. Here, Augustine wrestles with commanding his mind to act, but, because he's too weak and uncommitted, he fails to: "If" his desire to be chaste "were wholehearted," he writes, "it would not have to issue the command, it would already have willed it" (Wills, 177). And then, in sections 28–29, a pummeling "I" again hammers away. Still helpless, Augustine tries to stop the "great sheets of showering tears." He begins asserting control. He states several times that "I leaped," avoiding the passive "I was thrown." He leaps away from his friend, onto the ground, up to confront his fate. The actions are his. They are willed. The flailing about ends with "I blubbered pitiably" (181), but these tears reflect his self-motivation, *his* agency. Augustine is participating; *he's* con-verting. Just then a voice tells him to pick up the book and read; suddenly, his will and the text transform him.

Because these raw moments, recollected a decade after the ex-perience, are few, my sense is that the text is more written than remembered. Despite the moralizing hindsight, always inevitable, Augustine's *Confessions* becomes our first spiritually personal au-tobiography with glimmers of the memoirist's self-disclosure. I'll stipulate here (and unpack later) that the memoiristic begins to ignite when the depth of the emotion that the prose produces in the reader is as high-strung and sensorially felt as the author's por-trayal of his awe and fear during the act of writing itself. This is Augustine's stumbling upon (if not inventing out of whole cloth) the art of life-writing, his "churning and chafing," his clasping and unclasping, his tortuous delays and equivocations: "How long, how long—on the morrow is it, always tomorrow? Why never now? Why does this very hour not end all my vileness?" (181).

We remember that personal testimony is, by definition, the absence of corroborating evidence because what's being testified to is internal. The way we judge whether the author's inner con-dition is true is to gauge the authenticity of his yearning as literary discourse—narrative drama, metaphoric capture, descriptive zeal. A writer exaggerates emotions for us to feel them, to animate and overstay the moment's vitality. To strut and fret his hour—on the page. He stubbornly occupies the worded extension, transmutes the weight: jealousy, rage, misery, humility, closeness to God, or the sorrow of his dejection. Such is the autobiographical conceit no matter what the sufferer's life has been or will be.

ONE LAST thing to underscore about Augustine's "I." A written confession allows the author to create an "I" on the page, who *con-fesses* and who, as I've shown, should not be considered the writer's mirror but a separate character altogether. This "I" on the page becomes, as Eric Havelock (whom I also touched on earlier) says, "the 'personality' who could now discover its existence" *by way of writing* (114).[8] So: when Augustine says "I leaped," he's acting as his literary self. In effect, he becomes that self—an individual created by the writer as an entity who stands in for, stands up for, but cannot be, his actual self.

This narrator, who is saved in *Confessions,* is not the breathing, speaking, praying man Augustine was. All we have of the narrator is what the text gives us. The author is letting his narrator tell us certain things, leaving out, I assume, the most God-offending details of his lust. The autobiographical author is always a censor, the narrator, the censored.

Donald Morrill lays out a further twist on all this in his article "Character in Nonfiction."[9] The nonfiction writer creates the narrator. The narrator is the subject of the work who represents the writer. "We are invited," Morrill writes, "to wonder about the character of the nonfiction writer because we know he is interacting with his subject somehow." The real-life person wielding the pen is "not just acting upon" that "I." "He is wondering what the reader will also think about *his* character." Seeded inside this is the dramatic convention of the "fourth wall" behind which tellers like to hide: 'tis not me; 'tis the narrator I've asked to speak on my behalf. So: in memoir it's part of the critic's apparatus to question the veracity of who writers are *representing themselves as.*

The author is the creative force behind what the narrator says, while the narrator's tale, when it is superbly told, creates the illusion that the story is the narrator's alone. A felicitous sleight-of-hand. The idea is clarified by the scholar Roy Pascal. He describes why he considers *The Autobiography of St. Teresa of Avila* (1588), a work of penetrating devotion, is a rare multidimensional Christian confession.

> We see how her mind, submissive yet obstinate, trusting yet
> critical, wrestles with her visions, and how these themselves
> become surer, more understood in the sense that they find
> expression in practical behavior with others, ultimately in

the reform of conventual life and the founding of St. Joseph's [monastery].[10]

Pascal goes on to stress the "distinction of great autobiography." It is "not so much the truth of knowing as the truth of being, an integration and reunion of different aspects of the person, a coherence of the acting and the spiritual personality in the particularity of circumstances" (98).

Note well: *great autobiography* is distinguished by its *truth of being.*

Different aspects = the person who has fervently lived it and/or the person who is expressly putting the words down. The "truth of being" comes when our Jekylls and Hydes "wrestle" with each other toward "integration and reunion"—*reunion* is spot on—a coming together in language of what life has rent. Circumstances sever a person's coherence; writing (art) stitches the pieces back together. Call it as well a rapprochement between our carnal and soulful selves, the former, the way things are, the latter, the author's desire to change the way things are. The writing, again, is the fulcrum. It's not hard to imagine the soulful being in Augustine agenting the writer in him. This *I'll save you* narrator works on his behalf. Divided, he reunites himself—one "I" and another "I," same and different, the knitted spiritual personality. I stumble. I persevere. I weaken. I endure. I give in. I outlast the wretchedness of my concupiscence.

Still, one's being in writing is emblematic of what Michel Foucault labeled our modern condition. Hubert L. Dreyfus and Paul Rabinow analyze Foucault's sense of modernity, which commences in the 1780s and 1790s.[11] "Once the order of the world was no longer God-given and representable in a table," they write, "then the continuous relation which had placed man with the other beings of the world was broken. Man, who was once himself a being among others, now is subject among objects" (28). (God was a "being among others," and God as subject has also been displaced.) To lose one's locus with other beings is to become abjectly alone:

if Lord and Savior cannot come to the rescue, odds are we need to save ourselves.

As far as I know, Augustine is the first to record the fissure between himself and the Christian cosmos and (again, to his surprise) within himself—that I-and-Thou division of narrator and writer. Each individual, post-Enlightenment, is "not only a subject among objects," according to Dreyfus and Rabinow, but "the subject and the object of his own understanding" (28). Though it will take centuries, most shrouded in darkness, the ticking all but silent, Augustine's confessor will eventually become Camus's stranger.

JEAN-FRANÇOIS LYOTARD'S *The Confession of Augustine*, unfinished at his death in 1998, describes what makes up this book's compulsive metanarrative.[12] Lyotard argues that Augustine's antagonistic tone and caffeinated awakening are required of, and earned by, his effort. Indeed, "every single thing that he believes merits the lord's indignation is recorded," a "dossier for prosecution," as it were (95). Throughout *Confessions'* 141,520 words, Augustine must show that, in Lyotard's phrase, God's unceasing "violent affection" for him is reasonable. How? By showing how unworthy he is of God's love. He must be wholly abject, epitomize the hopeless sinner.

To be granted atonement, the author has to convince God that his worthlessness is somehow worthy. His worthiness comes via his writing. Lyotard argues that Augustine instructs God about the role of the author's craft in ameliorating humanity's sordidness: "Not only because these confessions make it clear to what extent his creatures have been poorly put together to be so unhappy, but also because he finds out to what perverse use writing can be turned, when it has been given to them by him" (95). In short, God gives us writing so we report just how tortured with scabs and lesions we are.[13] Multiply those scabs and lesions by psychotic episodes, and a perfervid author has to entrust his whole morbid life story to the page. There's no other way to psychic health.

Even after incomprehensible evils—the Crusades to recapture the Holy Land, the generational enslavement of Africans, the Holocaust—all within God's historical dominion, we still bow down in fealty and fear. This is why, according to Lyotard, the page-bound confession endures. This is why Christianity is indentured servitude. And yet backs whipped to shreds, feet and wrists nailed on planks, are never enough. Augustine's bondage is to be as embellished as it is celebrated.

Augustine, an artist-scholar and penitent sinner, was the first to insist in prose on his shame. But there is more to this than merely lifting his shirt and displaying his lashes. The revelation of sin and failure—Lyotard says that before God, Augustine is "one hundred percent guilty"—eventually careens out of control. Or better, that loss of control, when it's fiendishly unmoored, suggests that the author is improvising a new "I" on the page, if you will, one which he hopes will stabilize him as it harnesses an untapped aspect of himself.

Such self-creation, the opposite of Christian determinism, is engraved in the moment of composition when we assess our dilemmas and out comes *we know not what*. Writers may then examine the most vexing trait of their character, a golden nugget Lyotard coins: *What I am not yet, I am*.[14]

After Augustine, the attested-to infection of the self makes writers kowtow for centuries. The only two I know who fashion religious tracts equal to Augustine's dissonant sincerity are Thérèse of Lisieux (more on her presently) and Leo Tolstoy. Tolstoy arm-wrestles his "deconversion" story into print, in 1882, nearly fifteen hundred years after the bishop of Hippo.

I have some ideas why this weird gap exists.

One is that religious autobiographies, like the hymn "Amazing Grace," employ a potted plot: I'm lost, I'm pitiful, but I might still be saved. One Christian autobiography is, or at least reads, like any Christian autobiography. Augustine's is the prime directive, the seed from which each offspring grows. We have no other source. Nor do we get much challenging variety when we examine a handful of medieval and latter-day mystical authors; they form variations of, or exercises on, Augustine's admissions, despite their exhaustive, Stephen Kingish visions, hatched during or after self-punitive contemplation.

Literate evolution creeps along: alternatives to post-Augustine Christian sentimentality had to await genius: the plays of Shakespeare, the essays of Montaigne, the novel *Don Quixote* of Cervantes—all nondenominational, all the pinnacles of their forms. Strangely, too, it's not until 1782, the date of its publication, that we have the first secular autobiography, *The Confessions* of Jean-Jacques Rousseau. And a century later, Tolstoy's *Confession* comes out, a religious-spiritual-philosophical mashup whose goal is to free the author from Russian-bred Christian orthodoxy by throwing out its supernatural impulses and keeping its charitable heart, a true reformation of one's belief.

MY SUBJECT is the writer's ability to bring his spirituality into syntactic being. As the fountainhead, Augustine shows us the authoritarian pilings of confessional discourse, pilings that will undergird most future work. I think we've been braced enough by his craft and purpose to take a moment here, before discussing Tolstoy, to delineate the two forms of nonfiction, both written with an eye toward transcendence—the religious autobiography and the spiritual memoir.

An autobiography is *religious* when the author describes a journey he or she *has* lived—the path of a prescribed faith—and wishes his readers to follow. In Christian tales, this means dramatizing that one is born in sin, one accepts Christ as personal savior, and one works toward salvation through submission and prayer. Just as the Bible purports to be true because its scribes declare it is true, so, too, does the first-person autobiographer: What I say about myself is true because I say it's true.

The critic Albert E. Stone captures what is de rigueur in the religious autobiography: "The writer combines a vision of his whole life with a depiction of the embracing experience of *metanoia* [spiritual conversion], that complete transformation in which the ordinary time-bound self is lost in union with God."[15] Critics describe the Christian tell-all as a conversion narrative. The author confesses to an achieved set of beliefs, fired in the holy furnace of everyday coming-and-going and hammered into shape by a rigorous set of rules. Fine. But where does this change occur? In the occupation of the writer, obviously. But, for readers, this is evident only if we witness it, that is, feel it embodied in our lives because of the words we read. At a minimum, if the writing is honed and honest, readers accept that the author, prior to transcribing, was converted. The book is exhibit A, A for achievement. The claim resounds with, as Tom Wolfe used to say, "the simple fact that the reader knows *all this actually happened.*"

Augustine could not have written *Confessions*—*would* not have—unless *he* had been converted. I don't know about reborn; let's just say that because of praying in the garden and drafting the conversion as text, "his reluctance evanesced," the spring was rewatered. But remember: conversion is the climax. The life comes first, that is, his *unconverted* one. Conversion completes the perilous voyage. Thus, the religious autobiography does not end with redemption via hallucination, or divine abracadabra, that is, coming from outside the human will. Augustine is redeemed because as a writer he tells the story of *his* failure to understand God. That failure to understand God is his *understanding* of God, a lacquering we will encounter in three or four other notable Christian autobiographers.

Contemporary authors write autobiographically, of course, but when she, the author, focuses on a single subject, place, phase, relationship, or passion, we call it memoir. A memoir, in turn, is *spiritual* when the book deviates from the conversion model and pursues other experiential or psychic enthrallment, say, an author's quandaries about, or a need to comprehend, the afterlife, fate, chance, mysteries of being, the God of the gaps, the incorporeal, the baffling, the divine rapprochement—realms of affective not rational knowing, realms of involuntary alacrity, realms accessible often and only via the arts. Such realms are espied predominantly with the Hubble telescope of writing itself. Even if the ecstasy of the beyond is "experienced" in life, it still has to be "created" and *there* "experienced" in the author's hard-earned prose. You get no credit for living—the old saw goes.

In the last century, and proliferating in the last few decades, spiritual memoir has come into its diverse own. Some memoirists take this journey as they outgrow an astringent religion or their youthful enthrallment and arrive, dismayed, at the faith-fallen vexations of their adulthood—the *tales,* where women dominate, of Barbara Brown Taylor, Joe Mackall, Dani Shapiro, Joy Harjo, Hope Edelman, and Barbara Ehrenreich. Some explore that anxiety, emphasizing less their eucharistic flesh and more their intellectual gambits—the *testaments,* where men dominate, of John Henry Newman, Gandhi, Paramahansa Yogananda, Simone Weil, Thomas Merton, Malcolm X, and Fenton Johnson.[16] Some awaken after a faith-frantic childhood, parental brainwashing, or sexual abuse under religious auspices—the *deconversions* of Veronica Chater, Frank Schaeffer, Julia Scheeres, Ruth Wariner, and Kim Barnes.[17] Some rediscover their lapsed or rejected Christian convictions—the *reconciliations* of G. K. Chesterton and C. S. Lewis. Some begin nature treks, which, in turn, manifest inner spiritual wonders—the *pilgrimages* of Robert Pirsig, Peter Matthiessen, Paulo Coelho, Beverly Donofrio, Kathleen Norris, and Cheryl Strayed. Some go in quest of their enraptured selves in the woods or beside the sea or down a path of radical self-reliance—the *stations* of Emerson and Thoreau, Anne Morrow Lindbergh, Annie Dillard, Joan Anderson, Tom Montgomery Fate, and Mary Rose O'Reilley. And some ensoul themselves in the enigmas of faith— the *meditations* of the Christ-hunting Christian Wiman and the Catholic atheist-scientist Chet Raymo.

Now I want to gauge how Tolstoy's *Confession* handles this religious/spiritual divide. During his "spiritual crisis" of late middle age, he abandons union with God and devises his own spiritual individuation: *This is my creed, the creed I have secured, to spite the one religion handed me.* Despite the maverick's pique, Tolstoy's book bridges these opposing shores, and its singular fusion still reads like a memoir. His rabidly subjective and emotionally fraught narrator (always antsy, always paternalistic) shows us that he is sliding from one morally compromised faith into another. But, at least, it's *his* shift and, ultimately, a deconversion he can abide.

TWO THINGS are true about Leo Tolstoy in 1879. First, he had mostly given up on fiction, having published in the previous de-cade two titanic novels, *War and Peace* and *Anna Karenina*. The latter book exhausted him physically and morally: not long after its appearance, he termed the saga of adultery "an abomination." He found novel writing to be a poor substitute for confronting reli-gious issues and our existential lot. Second, because of his early tale-telling acclaim and the immoral lifestyle it had spawned and enabled, he was miserable. He was so ashamed of himself that post-*Karenina* his ambivalent atheism collapsed and he sought a new relationship to the "truth." He abdicated the throne of novelist and took up the mantle of religious critic—on the side of Christianity and against it.

Raised in the Russian Orthodox Church, Tolstoy lost his faith at eighteen. After years of debauchery up to age fifty, he wanted religion—or some source of intellectual security—back. In 1884, he published his *Confession*,[18] a retrospective analysis of the previous five years in which his midlife faith crisis un-balanced his literary and philosophical bearing. It is among the oddest of Christian tell-alls. Throughout, Tolstoy hungers for a soulful fortitude: "Is there any meaning in my life that wouldn't be destroyed by the death that inevitably awaits me?" (140). Readers note that Tolstoy's book title has no "a" or "the" attached. (There are no articles in the original Russian, but the absence in English is meaningful.) The singular noun by itself emphasizes its currency—that is, to find out what he *wants* to confess, he turns to this particular form of expression.

Early on in the book, he asserts, in defiance, that "Christian teaching plays no part in life; one never comes across it in one's relations with others and one never has to deal with it in one's own life" (116–17). He pegs believers as "stupid, cruel, and immoral people who think themselves very important" (117) He tags unbelievers as the finest people he knows: they have "intelligence, honesty, uprightness, goodness of heart, and morality" (117). He renounces orthodoxy in favor of "reading and thinking"—in essence, reason—and recalls that five years prior "my only real faith at that time was a faith in self-perfection" (119).

Of course, reason means progress, and progress, for an egoist like Tolstoy, entails an unchecked liberality in one's behaviors. At this, the young Tolstoy, an aristocrat and braggart, more than excelled. Here's part of his résumé:

> I killed people in war, I challenged people to duels in order to kill them, I lost at cards, I consumed the labor of peasants, I punished them, I fornicated, I deceived. Lies, theft, adultery of every kind, drunkenness, violence, murder. . . . There was no crime I did not commit, and for all this my contemporaries praised me and thought me a relatively moral man, as they still do. (121)

But the hyperobservant, me-first Tolstoy suffers a debilitating paranoia. He thinks that people ridicule him because of his alcoholic, adulterous, and arrogant excesses. He often imagines he's dying: the darkness is drawing close, and he must assign himself a purpose soon or else "nothing will remain but stink and worms" (134). (The death-obsessed Russian lived nearly thirty years after *Confession*.) At times, despair clings to his words like a rose vine. "You can only live as long as you're drunk with life; but when you sober up, you can't help but see that all this is just a fraud, and a stupid fraud. Precisely that: there's nothing even amusing or witty about it; it's simply cruel and stupid" (134). He says he doesn't know why the universe exists. He is tortured by the question. He wants it answered; he can't bear living in an untended and unintended cosmos.

By mid-book, Tolstoy's inquiry starts to change him—not just his focus but also his sensibility. To unburden his longing, he quotes Bible passages, an Indian sage, and nuggets from the saints and the martyrs—honoring now what he said earlier were useless "teachings of faith." He wonders if to feel secure all we need is the wisdom of the ancients. They have, he argues, lasted *this* long. His disclosures work him into a lather, and he declares that a pure belief in reason, without room for God as the Grand Sphinx, ends with insanity and suicide. A worrywart, Tolstoy plunges on with the tenor of a querulous depressive. Moreover, he shifts, as it suits him, the blame to those who should also feel his anguish: pagan nihilists, scientific rationalists, Orthodox dogmatics, jurisprudent bureaucrats—these last, the Ivan Ilyiches of the world. The only blameless one, he decides, is he who lives as Jesus lived. And yet, he counters, who can? It's impossible.

Tolstoy decides that no one is sincerer than the Christian peasant whose "irrational knowledge" paves the road to happiness. Irrational knowledge *is* faith, he posits. Peasants should know. (Though he aspires to join the class, Tolstoy is *not* one of them.) They are the "great mass of people, the whole of mankind." The nonindividuated mass, whom he lauds but who also rise, in his characterization, no higher than type. Uniformly, he writes in chapter 8, they believe God is "one and three," father, son, spirit, "creation in six days, devils and angels and everything I couldn't accept as long as I didn't go mad" (166).

There, as you hear, an odd admission—*as long as I didn't go mad*. What he needs to believe *in* is that which enables and surpasses his personal inclination. Such combat might drive anyone nuts. But peasant certainty empowers him, and he decides the masses know what's true. Not because Christianity has been their teacher but because the great and literate arbiter of truth, Tolstoy, will now promote their virtue, irrespective of church orthodoxy.

ON FIRST reading, Tolstoy's polemic seems to ape the Christian conversion set piece, as Augustine modeled it. However, after he weighs the possibilities of fault and blame, madness included, Tolstoy at last drapes the crucifix around his neck. One of his most perceptive biographers, Martine de Courcel, writes that with his confession/conversion he has, rather Christianly, "admitted his sins and proclaimed his faith."[19] Saved, he declares his actions from now on will embody his intentions—attend church, participate in sacraments, live frugally, leave his bourgeois habits, love God and peasant equally.

But wait. Opening salvation's door hardly calms his restlessness. Though Tolstoy says he erred less from wrong thought than bad living, the latter settles nothing. Try as he might, the self-cleansing fanatic cannot rid himself of his deviant past or his carping nature. He can neither forgive himself nor stop analyzing the demands of Christianity. He's insecure about Christ as savior or about any divine plan. The conundrum of belief, which is not preternatural, needs finer tuning.

Still, that conundrum splits him in two. Without God, Tolstoy has *lived* a lie of pain and deceit. He declares he is now, with God, living a life *free from* pain. But that's too easy. Resolving each query brings another—and more squirming. Biographer Courcel faults him. She writes that in "abandoning the dogmas of the Church, he thought he was freeing himself; in fact, he was about to become captive to the dogmas of his own making" (158). This is Tolstoy, the self-disappointment artist, his pattern, his personality. He confesses to convert (or converts to confess)—that is, he purifies religion down to what he declares valuable and cries, Eureka! But then he admits, often right away, that the conversion's center cannot hold. Statement and counterstatement cancel each other out.

The point here is that "the dogmas of *our* own making" come to writers because personal writing is testimony—what I affirm or deny becomes for me as scriptural as a sacred text becomes for others. The problem with Christian autobiography before Tolstoy is its overreliance on biblical reasoning. And yet the majority of confessors *after* Count Leo will find themselves authoring personal, not religious, not Bible-inspired revelation. Literary evolution anoints Tolstoy, not Augustine, the sire of spiritual memoir.

The final five chapters of *Confession* embroil his hemming-and-hawing conversion and deconversion. Tolstoy sides with Christianity only to oppose it, again and again, moving from found to lost, certain to vexed. What's remarkable is *not* his conversion but his evaluating his desire to convert as his confession.

Tolstoy's energy comes from his questions; they often crowd out or undermine his answers. His *tell* has power, though it's not the power we get from the dramatic narrative of a novel or a well-plotted contemporary memoir. It's something else. In *Confession*, we find no recourse to action or deed, no scenes, no reportage, no exchanges with others, and few anecdotes. Analysis trumps narrative. And yet it's not all rhetoric. There is a dialectic—a chess match in which Tolstoy plays himself. What's going on is a mélange of preaching virtues to the reader and arguing vices with himself, the self who can't figure out what, if anything, he should avow.

THE MORE I study *Confession*, the more apparent Tolstoy's conflicts become. (This is a sign that an erstwhile religious author is *turning* spiritual—nurturing his skepticism and enriching his rhetoric because he is interrogating a porous dogma.) On one hand, I fault Tolstoy for abandoning the drama of narrative propulsion. On the other hand, I also recognize the book he has written often aches with drama. To argue for uncertainty and to identify a faith-based deception in himself and in the Russian state was apostasy. Rarely did writers before or of this epoch—Mark Twain, Thomas Paine, and Jean-Jacques Rousseau aside—challenge religion's reign.

Several examples nail this *yes/but* figure of Tolstoy's hostility.

"To comprehend the truth one must not stand apart, and in order not to stand apart one must love and accept what one may not agree with" (191).

"In the Mass the most important words for me were: 'Let us love one another of one mind . . .' The following words, 'We believe in the Father, the Son and the Holy Spirit,' I omitted because I could not understand them" (192).

"How often I envied the peasants for their illiteracy and lack of education. The statements of faith, which for me produced nonsense, for them produced nothing false" (196).

And, "the more I began to be imbued with these truths [Christian teachings] I was studying and the more they became the foundation of my life, the more burdensome and painful these conflicts became and the sharper became the dividing line between what I didn't understand and what couldn't be understood except by lying to myself" (197).

We hear Tolstoy's constant undressing of orthodoxy—truths are "conflicts," "statements of faith . . . produce[d] nonsense," and belief is "interwoven by the thinnest of threads with lies" (196). It all repulses him.

Indeed, in the final pages of *Confession*, Tolstoy states that the church's teachings, which have enraged him into polemical denial, cannot be true. "But where did the falsehood come from," he writes, "and where did the truth come from? Both falsehood and truth had been handed down by what is called the Church. Both falsehood and truth are contained in tradition, in the so-called sacred tradition and holy writ" (202).

The only alternative is to leave, which he does, but not before his anti-Orthodox screeds continue to mount, as he privately prints and circulates another tirade, *A Criticism of Dogmatic Theology*. Eventually the church excommunicates him in 1901.

In 2013, Peter Carson's translations of *Confession* and *The Death of Ivan Ilyich* were published in one volume, from which I've been generously quoting. In her introduction, Mary Beard raises the problem any life-writer faces when her subject is turning personal misgivings into textual performance. "Autobiography is never quite transparent," Beard writes, "and . . . first-person spiritual memoirs are always partly constructions—retrospective and simplifying fictions imposed on the confusing stream of memories and on intellectual doubts and dilemmas" (22). That's so of any memoir: the writing often lowers one's elevation and quells one's dismay.

Beard's view, however, doesn't go very far. With Tolstoy, the core story is his confusion, his grappling with what's unresolved, his placing his "doubts and dilemmas" at the center of his soul's inquiry. Beard misses the point of the Russian's in-situ struggle as the struggle of literary writing itself. He's trying *not* to simplify his creed-crumbling vantage: he's confessing its intellectual trauma. That's why he's writing. If anything, Tolstoy is contending with his own unexamined views as a Christian—a doctrine both true and false for him—and it's that paradox which makes him so ornery or, if you like, a full-blooded Tolstoyan.

The real issue, I think, is rhetorical: How does one persuade others of what one values without listing unevidenced expository statements, whether agnostic or devout, which end up *sounding* simplistic, though they may not be simplistic at all?

I like Robert Jensen's tack in *Arguing for Our Lives:* "While faith experiences can be described to others, and patterns in faith experiences can be evaluated," he writes, "a faith experience is not evidence in the sense we use that term in intellectual life—it can't be replicated or presented to others to examine."[20] For many of us, faith is opinion, not fact. Faith is wished for, not verified. Christ was born of a virgin, crucified, and resurrected. Believe it or not. If you do believe it, those things *feel* like facts and, thus, make emotional sense. Imagine there's a videotape of the resurrection. We see the body (soul stowed inside) leave the tomb; the soul separates later in a "Caught on Camera" moment. Faith, however, exists where there *isn't* a videotape. It's *why* there's only a scriptural claim! If you accept it, you accept two things: one, that the Immaculate Conception "can't be replicated or presented to others to examine," and two, that such a conclusion is the province of its textuality.

Testaments of collective belief, ritualized in group pledges and accorded textual affirmation, take on the strange *actuality* of a religious event. Thus, avowing one's doctrine is (construed as) one's experience. When you admit, as Christians do, "I accept Jesus Christ as my personal savior," you've joined the tribe. In fact, the most secure bond of the tribe is its reliance on this ceremonial argot and discourse. In *Confession*, Tolstoy's great discovery is that when he had to assert Orthodox creeds, his contrarian nature was ignited. He couldn't suspend his disbelief. He had to write against rules he couldn't follow. Exploring the enigma of religious language—that what you say is true because you assert its tenets—led Tolstoy, in a sense, to give up on the idea that novels embodied the inner reality he was living. Fiction could no longer assuage his spiritual dryness—if it ever could. Antireligious and proconfessional exhortations, his forte as a writer for the rest of his life (the mid-1880s to his death in 1910), offered him a tonic to the most vexatious questions about how he or any of us should live.

FIFTEEN CENTURIES earlier, Augustine exsanguinated his body of sin, realigned himself with (and articulated) Christian teaching, and was, at last, compensated by the church with sainthood. Tolstoy, by contrast, wrestles with Christian discourse and rejects much of it in favor of his own salvational blueprint. He says he will be a better man when he serves the poor, abnegates attachment, and adopts peasant deprivations, many abject, some unattainable—but so be it. Such values will strengthen his self-reliance. Though he salvages Christ's call to social justice, Tolstoy is convinced that he, Tolstoy, originates a kind of post-Christian probity, one based as much on the man's aesthetic prowess as his new vision.

Like Kierkegaard, Tolstoy gives birth to an existential scrutiny of religion, which, unlike Kierkegaard, foregrounds rational argument over faith. He rejects the package: a church, an orthodoxy, and the political system that underpins it. Ever-free, ever-nosy, he denies that ideas and actions other than those native to his consciousness can change him. In effect, he spiritualizes himself. Tolstoy launches a proto-memoir whose opening gambit is to cast off the lies of the church and, in the ensuing journey, deprogram himself of the same.

In one sense, Tolstoy has turned his back on a millennium and a half of religious testimony without mentioning anyone by name. But there are hardly any *personal* authors he could turn his back on. Religious autobiography would need no Tolstoyan reformation had the church allowed its henpecked and censored writers—monastics and visionaries other than Augustine—to write of their inner selves on a par with their Christian vows.

Excepting the ur-Catholic Thomas Merton and the panreligionist Alan Watts, in America we've had few rebels as ferocious as Leo Tolstoy. In fact, much of the best writing on religion and spirituality, personal and otherwise, has been unrelentingly critical of the godly canon. Much beloved, C. S. Lewis's books on Anglicanism are works of intellectual Christianity, ships without sails in our time. To Lewis's consternation, many of the greatest writers of the last two centuries—Whitman, Dickinson, Freud, Darwin, Twain, Marx, Nietzsche, Conrad, Kafka, Woolf, Russell, Camus, Murdoch, Neruda, Fanon—have been antireligious or nonreligious *in the extreme*. Despite Flannery O'Connor, Walker Percy, Marilynne Robinson, Ron Hansen, and Anne Lamott in America and Roger Scruton and Don Cupitt in England, Christian themes in our literature are moribund, like coal deposits in Wyoming.[21] There, but unexcavated.[22]

These days, most memoirists center on experiential disbelief, where the self is the moral authority and divining arbiter of one's soul growth. The goal is to unfreeze the numinous, to parlay the sublime, to leave mysteries cliff-edged on ambiguity. This is not incongruent with Tolstoy, who, for the most part, killed off the religious autobiography, seemingly on blood thinners from the get-go. For contemporary writers, the most frequent question asked is, what is the psychic geography of my inner life? That's the door in each of us Tolstoy pushed open.

ॐ

WHERE ARE the women writers in the long onset of the male tell-all? Feminists—friends and scholars—have advised me that a woman's authorial sensibility and subject matter are different from a man's. To appreciate and clarify this difference, I note five Christian women (there are not many more prior to 1900) who enlisted priests to transcribe and edit their tales of ecstatic God-love: the German abbess Hildegard of Bingen (d. 1179), a composer of chants and three volumes of "visionary theology"; *A Book of Shewings to the Anchoress Julian of Norwich* (1393); *The Book of Margery Kempe* (1430s); *The Autobiography of St. Teresa of Avila* (1562–65); *The Autobiography of St. Thérèse of Lisieux: The Story of a Soul* (1898). It is unclear whether the women before Thérèse (who wrote in French) were literate in the vernacular or in the church's publishable script, Latin. It is clear that because they were women their work was expurgated.

Each woman is saddled with a "female" role in Christian confessionals, which, in the words of Jill Ker Conway,[23] "promoted meditation about the nature of God and the recording of direct experience of divine illumination" (12). The latter is most crucial. With women having no power or place in politics, law, or theology, areas in which they lacked agency, as Conway argues, a few joined the cloister to absorb and reflect the glorious beam. Men would describe their celestial visions during vagabondage or bookish devotion, but mysticism was reserved for, even *expected* of, women, who, at a minimum, had to be married to the church or Jesus or both.

Through this narrow gate, visionary women would relate their illuminations to a scribe—perhaps the first "as-told-to" examples of "celebrity" autobiography. (The sad backstory is that few women could write, let alone journal, fewer still had leave of their clerical and cleaning duties to produce confessions, and the lot had to have their work approved by a bishop—*nihil obstat* = nothing objectionable—before anything was printed.)

Margery Kempe is a kind of poster child for self-obliteration, tortured, as she is, by her (as she says) participation in Christ's crucifixion. She is the crying mystic who daily breaks down from any reminder or new vision of the Lord's travail. Her tale, third-person told, is termed a "self-biography":[24] "And she had such great compassion and such great pain, at seeing our Lord's pain, that she could not keep herself from crying and roaring though she should have died for it" (681).

Teresa of Avila tries to lodge the emotionally envisioned "other" in her convulsive prose, stealing some of Augustine's rhetorical hutzpah. As Juan of Avila, the church editor of her manuscript, remarked, "I think, too, these locutions have done your soul good, and in particular that they have made you see your own wretchedness and your faults more clearly, and amend them."[25] Whether his critique "helped" or not, Teresa's prose is often convincing. She writes of her spiritual mortification and its balm.

> I saw in his hand a long spear of gold, and at the iron's point there seemed to be a little fire. He appeared to me to be thrusting it at times into my heart, and to pierce my very entrails; when he drew it out, he seemed to draw them out also, and to leave me all on fire with a great love of God. The pain was so great, that it made me moan; and yet so surpassing was the sweetness of this excessive pain, that I could not wish to be rid of it. The soul is satisfied now with nothing less than God. The pain is not bodily, but spiritual; though the body has its share in it, even a large one. It is a caressing of love so sweet which now takes place between the soul and God, that I pray God of His goodness to make him experience it who may think that I am lying.[26]

I admire Teresa's bravura at the end, defending her testimony against anyone who thinks she's lying, hardly a submissive stance. I also like the originality of her Janus-faced emotion. *The sweetness of this excessive pain* feels authentically sensual. Is there any way *not* to read this as religious/female erotica? Perhaps, less salacious, it's how radiant pain/pleasure in the body *feels* as it's captured, held, and slips away. This, which male authors also portray, color-fasts one of my threads, namely, that superbly wrought prose—the thrill of the story and its sublime insights—may enact a similar experience in the reader.

Two caveats.

First, in Teresa's *Autobiography* and her imperious how-to *The Way to Perfection* (1567), she describes, with authority and ardor, her visions. But her descriptive flush is not enough. She must also make her tale sound *exemplary*, push readers—nuns and monks and other human beings—to follow the Christ route as virtuously as she has. Desiring such a life—humility, devotion, obedience, self-reproach—I call the *exemplary conceit*, the pious writer's selfless tract that is, ultimately, meant to net others. (Humility and selflessness are dicey virtues, susceptible to grandstanding by anyone. To write authentically of one's extreme zeal for God is to focus more on the lover, the "I," than the loved. This is not a bad thing; in fact, it is one of the doors through which the spiritual memoir will eventually emerge.)

Second, to the contention that the five Christian women listed above share "female" as a separate life-writing identity from males', I'm on the fence. Mary Mason argues in "The Other Voice: Autobiographies of Women Writers" that medieval female autobiography is not about the Augustinian "battle of opposing forces . . . where a climactic victory for one force—spirit defeating flesh—completes the drama of the self." Rather, she continues, "the self-discovery of female identity seems to acknowledge the real presence and recognition of another consciousness, and the disclosure of [a] female self is linked to the identification of some 'other.'"[27]

Yes, Augustine pits flesh against spirit. Yes, most authors in Augustine's as well as Teresa's time were men. (I also don't want to discount the letter-writers, many of whom were female.) And yes, we are uncomfortably close to casting women's visions as imagined (the vile word was *hysterical*) and, thus, discountable. Gender divisions apply. But, to Mason's argument, can we really say that Augustine does not engage his own "other," who is God, a male figure who confounds him, in whom he seeks union and whom he so fears offending that his dread of same instigates Augustine's change? True, Augustine and Teresa (both sainted) search different neighborhoods (he lusts for a woman, she lusts for a spirit) where the deity is ensconced. But their destinies parallel; both build and cross a bridge to the supernal spirit, the most personal of relationships.

The estimated *illiteracy* rates in pre-Shakespearean England, about 1550 (I assume this is roughly equivalent to those in Spain), are 98 percent for women and 90 percent for men. By 1900, these rates drop to 5 percent.[28] Even in Renaissance England, few women could read, let alone write autobiography. Even if their subject matter, say, in letters, was the "other," for example, a relationship with a husband, family, or children—eyeing not her but their personal fulfillment—we still don't have enough of their work to evaluate how women's religious confessions might read differently from men's.

I trust my critique will not be seen by feminist scholars as a copout. I think, however, that the most reliable evolution of religious/spiritual writing follows not a gendered hegemony but one based on the writer's literariness—direct address, songful portrayal, authentic witnessing, narrative depth. Such work appeals to readers who ache for direction from those most like them, who sound an overtly personal knell.

OUT OF a handful of medieval women writers, the exemplary conceit spirals into neurosis if the author's soul ambitions overtake all—as is the outcome in Thérèse of Lisieux's *The Story of a Soul*.[29] Thérèse, a late nineteenth-century wunderkind, is among the most hallowed of Catholic writers, in part because her white-hot Christ-rapture was extinguished at twenty-four by tuberculosis and because no one has ever matched the fanaticism of her God-love.

An unalloyed religious calling in one so young is extremely rare. It begins at four (Thérèse's first trip to Lourdes) and continues at seven (first communion), at ten (first "trembling hallucinations" of the Blessed Virgin), at thirteen (first visionary headaches), and at fifteen (postulant in the Lisieux Carmel Order). Her conversion is intensified with directives from her mother prioress, who had heard Thérèse's "childhood memories" and insisted she write them down. Soon, Thérèse receives the habit and the veil, begins journaling, and becomes, at seventeen, the "Child Bride" of Christ, whom she calls her "Divine Spouse."

Thérèse writes generously, cloyingly, and frantically of the halcyon freedom of living inside priory walls. She describes her happy faith as "the way of spiritual childhood," innocence and trust and surrender. Moreover, she holds her consumption dear, for it mimics Christ's scourge. The toll of her joy and inner lacerations lead her to suffer scruples, that is, "religious melancholy," a trial of the soul. (Scruples, often likened to pebble-filled shoes, racked men and women equally.) The character-building condition, she declares, is too painful for words. Any reader of her tale "would have to pass through this martyrdom to understand it well, and for me to express what I suffered for *a year and a half* would be impossible" (84).

Often this is her tack: to say, "there are no words." But that doesn't stop her from filling her journal. When, as a tubercular, she coughs up blood ("a bubbling stream mounting to my lips"), she deputizes her pen to personify her own blood as that of her divine suitor. She writes how she "was interiorly persuaded that Jesus, on the anniversary of His own death, wanted to have me hear His first call. *It was like a sweet and distant murmur that announced the Bridegroom's arrival*" (210–11). Blood gurgling in her throat marks his coming, and Christ begins healing her from within. The gift she receives is more than a keening voice. It's a literary prowess, a brash confidence seldom heard in a male or a female disciple. It's elemental to her that she converses with Christ in prose.

In her final years, Thérèse, despite the blood in her phlegm, transfers her physical torment into a kind of medicinal exhortation that wipes out the pain. What's more, her free-flowing meditations and diary entries invite God to participate in *her* embodiment of him through an enraptured hyperbole. She metamorphoses Christ's indiscernibleness into language. She animates Jesus to watch over the "little souls" like her with transmogrifying commands, so that he regards them as immolated victims! "O my God! Will Your Justice alone find souls willing to immolate themselves as victims? Does not Your *Merciful Love* need them too?" (180).

Thérèse beseeches Christ to acknowledge her ardent desire and, strangely, as if his were derelict, to reciprocate hers. She stalks his presence and absence without animus. And yet she paints him as playing too hard to get or, worse, an indolent messiah.

"As long as You desire it, O my Beloved, Your little bird will remain without strength and without wings and will always stay with its gaze fixed upon You. It wants to be *fascinated* by Your divine glance. It wants to become the *prey* of Your Love" (200).

And, "I beg You to cast Your Divine Glance upon a great number of *little* souls," like her. "I beg You to choose a legion of *little* Victims worthy of Your LOVE!" (200).

And! "Never let me be a burden to the community, let nobody be occupied with me, let me be looked upon as one to be trampled underfoot, forgotten like Your little grain of sand, Jesus" (275).

It shouldn't be hard to *hear* Thérèse beefing up her words with violent referents and galvanizing her tone with capitalized pronouns, emphatic italics, and chesty demands that sing, accuse, infer, and joust, especially on the ironical word *little:* Oh, please notice how small but, by writing to You so passionately of my smallness, how worthy I am.

THÉRÈSE'S THE *Story of a Soul* documents her passion for Christ. She ignites and tends the "Fire of Desire" with penitential language that makes wild, erotic, and near-psychotic claims. In her defense, several of her siblings and those at her canonization testify to her suffocating goodness. For us, however, the problem is, how much credence do we grant the tale? Does it matter that we believe? I think it matters because such severe interiority begets our incredulity. Instead of being inspired by or participating in such a story, we spend our time arguing with her reliability.

How should we read what is wholly private, inner, unverifiable? An author claiming that we should *believe* her work begets questions of persuasion and honesty. We have to balance the rational and the ecstatic elements of life-writing; neither should exploit or censor the other. The more tangible the ecstasy described, the more we believe it. But such stories have power in their relevance: How we apply the author's discoveries and purpose to our lives is always in play. It's not immoderate to say that if more people, more women, *wanted* what Thérèse says she pursued and sometimes grasped, they would follow her, right? But virtually no one does.

It seems that her summit is to have (to be seen for having) that which Christian doctrine burdens the Virgin Mary with—not a mirror of conflicted human love but an exemption from human imperfection. Thérèse's purpose in writing her story, part nunnish and part freakish, is to jettison herself as far from our mulish existence as possible. Why? So: she joins the holiest of mortals, earns the church's highest award. Indeed. The church dispensed with its fifty-year rule for postdeath canonization, and Thérèse was sainted in 1925, twenty-eight years after her death.

In a sense, the link she couples between her and her savior is no more than a ruse, calculated madness, the more outlandish the tale, the more likely the divinity. It sounds devious. But there it is—*in writing*. Like any skilled artisan, Thérèse fashions metaphoric, metaphysic, and argumentative schemes into a cantata-like testament, which because it has been set in print must, like the Lives of the Saints, be true.

Is such the end point, a fantasy of exhaustion that turns a faithful tell-all into one worthy of God's notice? As the twentieth century begins, this ancient ameliorative confession reaches a rhetorical zenith—only the most mad, obeisant, dying-of-the-light

authors transmute what the putatively bullying and deeply needy
Jesus Christ wants.

Still, I can't help but admire the metaphorical and sensual
varnish of her style. It is confiding, intimate, and ragingly personal. Hers are words one *writes*, not words one *speaks*, though
in her poetic heart she purrs to Christ, a Juliet of the night. This
I-in-You, You-in-Me current possesses qualities we respond to
rhetorically—the highest drama of devotion, emotions washed
purer than snow.

What do I think Thérèse is trying to convey?

First is the primacy of her relationship to her beloved Savior, a devotion that shines more brightly on her than on him.
Second, and more crucial, is the primacy of the Thérèse-Christ
relationship as textually incarnate. Written by God or the faithful, the Word incarnated is true. "The Word of the Lord shall
abide forever." With Thérèse, though, there's a big difference.
In her autobiography, no God, no Hebrew scribe, no post-Jesus
apostle, no Roman historian is authoring the sacred. Thérèse
is. If her pillow talk is her experience—and let's take her *at her
word*—then she adds emotional weight and witness to a series of
precepts: (a) God is good; (b) her surrender to God is also good;
(c) and her surrender produces a profound psychological stability
for Thérèse; in a phrase, she earns a master's in piety.

God is good, and to adhere to that goodness is to be *nearly*
as good as God. Moreover, all this exemplifies the Christian passion: suffering the unrequited love of Christ, Thérèse's dying to live
characterizes the essence of her religion.

For the writer to present the enormity of her soul in the radical revelation that her soul and its enormity have been determined
by the divine intervention of Jesus Christ in the world is—if I can
hold onto that notion with the weight it deserves—unfathomable.
And yet I do realize that there are few other ways to render that
enormity than discursively, as holier-than-thou, as beyond our
kith and ken, life as performance art, an exhibitionism of circus-
like spectacle, the nun who burns herself in the public square of

her prose. Such is the legacy of Thérèse's 1898 self-immolating story.

PLENTY LAUDATORY has been inked about Thomas Merton's *The Seven Storey Mountain*,[30] published in 1948 when its author was thirty-three and had, six years prior, joined the Abbey of Gethsemani in Kentucky to become a Cistercian monk. It was the fulfillment of a lifelong wish, which Merton, in the tale, slowly recognizes in himself and which, he says, his omniscient God alerted him to in careful installments. His autobiography is a complexly onerous and highly unstable book. Overlong and I-dominant (a bit less stridently self-infatuated than Thérèse), its 423 pages sweep through Merton's childhood, adolescence, and young adulthood. The first half is studded with his literary flirtations and religious concerns, reading medieval mystics and Gerard Manley Hopkins—and praying at the abbey, where he often tells us he is writing this very book. In 1938, after graduating from Columbia University, he hears the whispers of faith coming from a nearby Catholic church. Alchemized by the Mass, he wants to be a Catholic. Merton atones for his youthful embarrassments as he converts, is baptized, covets the priesthood, and leaves his bookish friends and university teaching for the contemplative life. All this clockwork religiosity also makes way for his other calling—that of the writer who harbors spiritual potential.

I will not dwell on the book's flaws—Merton himself said in 1967 that were he to revise the book, one of America's best-selling religious books ever published, "I'd cut out a lot of the sermons, I guess, including the sales pitch for Catholic schools."[31] I agree. Catholic righteousness barges into his prose like militarized police at a peace rally. About the monks' sway, he can be pretentious. At a Gethsemani liturgy he attends in 1942, the war in Europe and Japan newly joined, he notes that the "eloquence" of these ultrapious men praying in a room in Kentucky constitutes "the center of all the vitality that is in America." What's more, the smitten Merton declares, such "is the cause and reason why the nation is holding together. . . . They are winning for [the country] the grace and the protection and the friendship of God" (*Mountain*, 325).

Still, despite the puffery, no reader escapes Merton's forthright love of Catholicism, a pull almost unthinkable during the Second World War, what with malaise-ridden existentialists at his heels. In retaliation to Sartre and (godless) communism, Merton tends his faith via reason and revelation.

Merton's most powerful revelation comes during a visit to Cuba. There, where the church holds sway over the masses, he feels so free that he writes "the first real poem I had ever written," which he quotes in the text. (It's curious that the Catholic milieu stirs his bookish gifts. Merton's collected poetry will total more than one thousand pages.) At a Mass in the Church of St. Francis at Havana, during the consecration, he watches a group of raucous children asserting "Creo en Dios," *I believe in God*. The effect on him is like Beethoven hearing Mozart. Merton has "a realization of God made present by the words of Consecration in a way that made Him belong to me."

He continues: "But what a thing it was, this awareness: it was intangible, and yet it struck me like a thunderclap." And: "It was the light of faith deepened and reduced to an extreme and sudden obviousness." Merton boards the spiritual transport.

> The reason why this light was blinding and neutralizing was that there was and could be simply nothing in it of sense or imagination. When I call it a light that is a metaphor which I am using, long after the fact. But at the moment, another overwhelming thing about this awareness was that it disarmed all images, all metaphors, and cut through the whole skein of species and phantasms with which we naturally do our thinking. It ignored all sense experience in order to strike directly at the heart of truth, as if a sudden and immediate contact had been established between my intellect and

the Truth Who was now physically really and substantially before me on the altar. But this contact was not something speculative and abstract: it was concrete and experimental and belonged to the order of knowledge, yes, but more still to the order of love.

Another thing about it was that this light was something far above and beyond the level of any desire or any appetite I had ever yet been aware of. It was purified of all emotion and cleansed of everything that savored of sensible yearnings. It was love as clean and direct as vision: and it flew straight to the possession of the Truth it loved.

And the first articulate thought that came to my mind was: "Heaven is right here in front of me: Heaven, Heaven!"

It lasted only a moment. (283–85)

Here is spiritual arrival and evanescence, complicated and clarified in language. First, Merton, the witness, says that God is "made present by the words of the Consecration." Intoning God in/with words produces God. Next, Merton, the critic, says "light" is and is not a metaphor. It's the "light" of faith, which doesn't shine but does declare. In addition, though he "saw" with the "light," what he saw wasn't ocular. Same with the "heart of truth," another metaphor. There's no escape. Merton, as much ironist as disciple, has to try and describe that which words can't quite describe.

Last, Merton, the paradoxer, depicts the "light" as what he's always longed for, and yet the "light" is purified of yearning: *It flew straight to the possession of the Truth it loved.* How does light fly? Poetically. I should say *only* poetically. To get the Truth to what *it* loves requires writing. (I say this from *my* passion for writing and spirituality—and because I'm reminded that millions of people are easily terrified every day by our mere existence. Their fears are non-language-based and don't need the writer's art *to be real.*) This sharpest of memories produces in Merton a "first articulate thought": This Is Heaven! There all along. But only now can he see it.

These are among the most genuine passages in Merton, where he is *writing spiritually*. He embodies the fact and the memory and their meaning in prose, then says that prose can't portray all that, then says that the very thing prose can't portray must, nonetheless, culminate in an "articulate" thought, that is, a *worded* one, which, it turns out, is synonymous with heaven—a word that names the place or defines the state which the spiritual intuition gives birth to.

For me, it would have been literature. For Merton, it's the Catholic Mass.

The jolt, he feels, will sizzle for the rest of his life—in prayer and contemplation, in the offices of the church, in solitude. He will live in the *light* of that light, expect and hope the shining happens again via the repetition of a monk's rituals and duties as well as those of a priest (he took solemn vows in 1947) he will fulfill thousands of times. "The strange thing about this light," Merton writes, "was that although it seemed so 'ordinary' in the sense I have mentioned, and so accessible, there was no way of recapturing it" (285). And yet he does, at least this one time in Cuba, edge into the numinous, dwell there briefly, hatch a way to write of it, which, in turn, hatches myriad other ways—especially in diary entries, letters, poems, and personal essays—to write of what is so accessible and so uncapturable. For Merton, the experience unlocks one of the more esoteric of the Catholic mysteries: the way God works with the literary man—out from and back into words.

WHILE MERTON becomes quite articulate on Catholic theology (one reason the church lets a Cistercian keep writing and publishing) through the rest of the book, nothing holds a candle to his soul-alarm in Havana. The whole story rises to and falls away from this apex, like the heroine's aria in a musical. Stephen Sondheim once said that in order to write a good song he needed to write the play first so the narrative would present him with a climactic moment his heroine had to sing of her joy or despair. Perhaps Merton's autobiography exists for him, like a five-act play, to centerpiece his Havana revelation. All this suggests that Merton's Catholicism is spiritual because its incarnate truth arrives but rarely.

I'm reminded of another pearl from Merton: "As long as we are in this world, our life in Christ remains hidden."[32] What kind of a Christian are you if your life in Christ "remains hidden"? This is Merton's manna: Mass in Havana is a breakthrough—he ate that day, but the meal didn't end his hunger. The spiritual path, according to Merton, is one of random tremors, unpredictabilities. The individual's constant supplication for grace means that grace is not common. (What makes it *grace* is that it is given, not requested.)

What makes Merton continuously interesting is that he is not saved by such insights. As for Augustine, sixteen centuries before him, salvation hardly curbs his dissatisfaction—or his need to write. Off to his cloister room he goes, to pray and study in silence, and to write, so his "life in Christ" is *less* hidden, though he remains sentenced to "this world." For Merton, "this world" amounts to the Abbey of Gethsemani, in rural Kentucky, surrounded by an eight-foot-high concrete-block wall. Despite its remoteness and its maxim, "God Alone," carved into its portal, the monastery is *not* heaven. And, as Merton surmised early on, pursuing the idyllic directly means you can't have it.

Again, I think the elemental question for Merton is how writing helps him hunt down his desired "life in Christ," even as he says it's absent or unattainable. Is this why he had to write—and publish—so much? Were his poems and essays and literary criticism and his Christian philosophy mere exercises in futility?

Some in the legion of Merton scholars see him, in degree of accomplishment, as a poet, a memoirist, an essayist, a letter writer, a diarist, a cultural critic, and only then a contemplative Catholic or a nascent Zen Buddhist. This ranking seems right to me. Multiple times he tells us in *The Seven Storey Mountain* that he *wants* to be, will be, a writer. While a student at Columbia in the late 1930s, he and his classmates were "furiously writing novels." One of Merton's is a "long stupid novel about a college football player who got

mixed up in a lot of strikes in a textile mill" (181–82). The writer/
critic Mark Van Doren tells Merton, whose hermeneutic skills are
impressive, to teach literature, or at least try it, before monasti-
cism. Merton reads medieval philosophy, lingers on St. Ignatius
Loyola's *Spiritual Exercises*, and writes his thesis on William Blake.

He persists with his dream, declaring midway through his autobiography, "I wanted to be a writer, a poet, a critic, a professor." He wants intellectual pleasures but suspects these will end
in "spiritual disaster." He blames himself for his appetites, one
of which is "the gratification of one's own ambitions," where he is
mired in "his own internal self-idolatry." Merton's dowdy assessment is that "because I was writing for myself and for the world, the
things I wrote were rank with the passions and selfishness and sin
from which they sprang" (231). In his early twenties, Merton submits a novel for publication, but it's rejected. Then, in Havana, he
writes his "first real poem." He pens more fiction, letters, a journal,
and translates medieval French texts. Even if he becomes a monk,
he feels he need not relinquish his literary calling.

When he packs his bags for Gethsemani in December 1941,
he burns his three and one-half novels. And yet he declares that
writing "was born in me and is in my blood. . . . I brought all the
instincts of a writer with me into the monastery, and I knew that
I was bringing them, too. It was not a case of smuggling them in.
And Father Master [his abbot, Dom Frederic Dunne] not only
approved but encouraged me when I wanted to write poems and
reflections and other things that came into my head in the novitiate" (389).

And then, surprise, he submits his poetry to New Directions
press, they publish *Thirty Poems*, and he, still a novice, receives a
copy in the mail near the end of 1944:

> By this time I should have been delivered of any prob-
> lems about my true identity. I had already made my simple
> profession. And my vows should have divested me of the
> last shreds of any special identity.

But then there was this shadow, this double, this writer who had followed me into the cloister.

He is still on my track. He rides my shoulders, sometimes, like the old man of the sea. I cannot lose him. He still wears the name of Thomas Merton. Is it the name of an enemy?

He is supposed to be dead.

But he stands and meets me in the doorway of all my prayers, and follows me into church. He kneels with me behind the pillar, the Judas, and talks to me all the time in my ear.

He is a business man. He is full of ideas. He breathes notions and new schemes. He generates books in the silence that ought to be sweet with the infinitely productive darkness of contemplation.

And the worst of it is, he has my superiors on his side. They won't kick him out. I can't get rid of him.

Maybe in the end he will kill me, he will drink my blood.

Nobody seems to understand that one of us has got to die. (410)

Merton goes on to publish some fifty books during his lifetime, from his thirtieth to his fifty-third year. More come out posthumously.

To further the discussion I began with Augustine, Merton finds that his "I," the writer, authorizes the "I," the narrator (whom some call a character or a persona) on the page.[33] We have in Merton a monk-versus-writer tension, more expansively and psychologically shaped than in his autobiographical Christian forebears. With Augustine, the religious persona is attested to; with Tolstoy, the religious persona is disputed; with Merton, the religious persona is a struggle between contentious becomings: that which he wants to be and that which he has become but whose indefiniteness he retains. Sometimes Merton the monk wants to be the writer; other times Merton the writer wants to be the monk. There's no telling exactly who's who or who exactly is showing up on the page. The two are a moveable feast. Again, Jean-François Lyotard's paradox fits: *What I am not yet, I am*—neither "I" Merton employs, writer or monk, is ever fully separate or fused.

I DISAGREE that *The Seven Storey Mountain* should be prized for its religious/spiritual value than its writerly artistry. That artistry and Merton's eloquence make the work disarmingly honest and adroitly aesthetic. At book's end, Merton, shifting to third person, dramatizes his Gethsemani-birthed ambivalence. Once the gate closes, he's sure he wants to be there but not sure in what capacity: continue writing poems and articles for magazines or be a contemplative—the former his nature, the latter his choice. What should "I," whose disposition is to write, do? What should "he," the contemplative, do? For counsel, Merton enlists the aid of the abbot, maybe to stroke his ego, maybe to nurse his vulnerability. Dom Frederic tells him, "I want you to go on writing poems" (413).

Permission given, Merton makes the most of it. In addition to fashioning his Catholic persona on the page, he commands God to command Merton, who's granted God the first-person pronoun, to let him, Merton, have it. Here is the book-ending trope, a page-long passage, which Merton renders with italics and inside quotation marks.

He has God (I) tell Merton (You):

> ". . . you shall taste the true solitude of my anguish and my poverty and I shall lead you into the high places of my joy and you shall die in Me and find all things in My mercy which has created you for this end." (422–23)

What's phenomenal about *The Seven Storey Mountain* are these and other acts of Merton's shape-shifting prose. His autobiography pushes back at the Augustinian confession, which ends in an obediently bent and climactically saved individual. Merton's not that man. His is not a record of polemical exhaustion into faith. His is a new gambit in life-writing: one who repeats the following verse and chorus: the light comes, you live in the light, and the light goes away. This is so not by my precept but by Merton's originality. All of it future-focused: I shall lead you, you shall taste, you shall die, you shall find, etc. What is coming *is* what has been found. Beginning in 1948, Merton's work is strong enough to move him in new directions as well as to integrate the monk's and the artist's calling. Such a talent no other religious author I know of before Merton comes close to.

Merton is not Augustine. He seems, instead, to be both partners in a dance: the literary Merton asks the converted Merton why the literary Merton remains bent on communicating—to himself, his Gethsemani brothers, and us—who this self-ennobling monastic is and why he needs these two personas, monk (contemplative) and writer (activist), to unite, why both keep contending for control of his psyche.

Merton's probing meditations, his spellbound poems, his rapturous criticism—all these things beacon millions to read him but few (fewer today than ever in the moribund monasteries of America) to follow him. I think the severity of his Kentucky withdrawal is the strongest impediment to people wanting to "be like Tom." *The Seven Storey Mountain* bears such a vibrant, perspicacious intelligence on the page that the hermit's life, which Merton says indulges the inner light, is overstated. Removing himself from society did nothing to take the culture of books away. It made him more bookish than he'd already been. Which was a lot. Books were his mistress. No wonder Merton, age fifty-three, having read extensively about Buddhism, traveled to Asia to visit monasteries in India and Thailand; he died of a freak electrocution while at a conference in Bangkok. The question haunts us long after his death: Would he have stayed in the East? This 1954 letter to his abbot gives an idea.

> I am beginning to face some facts about myself. Yes, need for more of a life of prayer, greater fidelity, greater sincerity and simplicity in doing what God wants of me. Easy to say all that. It depends on getting rid of something very deep

and very fundamental in myself. . . . Continual, uninter-
rupted resentment. I resent and even hate Gethsemani. I
fight against the place constantly. I do not openly allow myself—not consciously—to sin in this regard. . . . I am not
kidding about how deep it is. It is DEEP.[34]

An eremitical life is exemplary of nothing but preference.
Would Austen, Dostoevsky, Chekhov, or Toni Morrison have been
better writers had they been more Mertonesque? One need not be a
Christian to value or ape his literariness. This is what I mean when
I say a good spiritual writer achieves his value (far) more through
the artist's aesthetic than through religious conviction. If the reverse were true, then such writing would have a pedigree by now
and Merton would be one of thousands. But that lineage has not
evolved. And, if humans on occasion augur the divine, spirit-kept
and set-apart, as I think Bach and Bob Dylan are, then Merton is
divine as well.[35]

NOTES

1. Perhaps the two most authoritative studies about the Bible as literature are Northrop Frye's *The Great Code: The Bible and Literature* (New
York: Harcourt, Brace, Jovanovich, 1982) and Harold Bloom's *The Shadow
of a Great Rock: A Literary Appreciation of the King James Bible* (New Haven:
Yale University Press, 2011).

2. How rare for any character or narrator in the Bible to demonstrate—
as opposed to moralize about—his or her interior life. Christ's purported
doubts are an exception. How rarely the anxieties of the book's participants
are honestly confronted by those participants themselves. This is one of
many reasons why I believe the Bible, a mythic text, fails the *literary* test.

3. Augustine, *Confessions*, trans. Garry Wills (New York: Penguin
Classics, 2006). In his commentaries on four of the twelve books of *Confessions*, published separately, Wills—whose translation has a luminescent
poetry all its own—labels Augustine's masterpiece *The Testimony*, a curious
alternative title. The word *confession* has to do with avowing what is private and, often, shameful, while testimony, in our parlance, is evidence
given under oath by experts or eyewitnesses supporting the actuality of a
claim. Testimony is also an open acknowledgment of one's faith.

One difference between the two words involves where (on the witness stand, in a book, in a confessional) and to whom one is admitting the "truth." For Augustine, it is to God; for the rest of us, it may be to God, but it may also be to a family, an identity, a culture, ourselves: the testimony of the private self in a written document, typically intended for publication. Moreover, to confess necessitates a confessor, a listener-absolver.

As I suggest, some of the most moving passages in Augustine are those pleadings with himself, holding himself accountable for not loving God more than he does and for not loathing himself sufficiently. For me, this splitting of the self in writing so that one self, the moralistic author, upbraids the other self, the hapless sinner, for his wickedness is beyond confession or testimony. It's a form of self-persecution.

4. Alan Watts, *Buddhism: The Religion of No-Religion: The Edited Transcripts* (Boston: Charles E. Tuttle, 1996), 69.

5. Wills notes in *Saint Augustine's Conversion*, "I translate all Scripture texts from the Latin version Augustine used." Garry Wills, *Saint Augustine's Conversion* (New York: Viking Penguin, 2004), xiii.

6. Marjorie O'Rourke Boyle, "Religion," in *Encyclopedia of Rhetoric* (New York: Oxford University Press, 2001).

7. Michael W. Higgins, "Lecture 2: The Confessions of Saint Augustine," in *From Augustine to Chesterton and Beyond: Great Spiritual Autobiographies* (Rockville, MD: Now You Know Media, 2015).

8. Ibid.

9. Donald Morrill, "Character in Nonfiction," *TriQuarterly* (October 25, 2011), http://www.triquarterly.org/craft-essays/character-nonfiction. My analysis of Morrill's *The Untouched Minutes*, a memoir that plays with dueling narrator-selves, originally appeared in the *Oxford American*, no. 78 (August 2012), http://www.thomaslarson.com/publications/essays-and-memoirs/241-shifting-self.html.

10. Roy Pascal, *Design and Truth in Autobiography* (Cambridge, MA: Harvard University Press, 1960), 98. Roy Pascal's is the most insightful study I know about the grand old form of autobiography. It's available again as an ebook.

11. Hubert L. Dreyfus and Paul Rabinow, *Michel Foucault: Beyond Structuralism and Hermeneutics* (Chicago: University of Chicago Press, 1983).

12. Jean-François Lyotard, *The Confession of Augustine*, trans. Richard Beardsworth (Stanford: Stanford University Press, 2000).

13. In *The Swerve* (New York: W. W. Norton, 2011), Stephen Greenblatt disputes this notion (from chap. 8, "The Way Things Are"): "The idea that language was somehow given to humans, as a miraculous invention,

is absurd. Instead, Lucretius wrote, humans, who like other animals used inarticulate cries and gestures in various situations, slowly arrived at shared sounds to designate the same things. So too, long before they were able to join together to sing melodious songs, humans imitated the warbling of birds and the sweet sound of a gentle breeze in the reeds and so gradually developed a capacity to make music" (192).

14. This is my favorite quotation on autobiography and memoir. First, Lyotard's statement most of us see as valid: human psychology is twofold: we are the person we hope to become and the person we are right now. Or, for this book, in the space between "what I am not yet" and "what I am" there is struggle. That struggle with being here and not yet being here is the space of the spiritual.

15. Albert E. Stone, "The Soul and the Self," in *Autobiographical Occasions and Original Acts: Versions of American Identity from Henry Adams to Nate Shaw* (Philadelphia: University of Pennsylvania Press, 1982), 81.

Written before the memoir age, Stone's survey of autobiography is prodigious. He's read them all; he understands the form's emphasis on difference, on "versions" of identity. No matter how tedious the prose, he finds the shifting American selfhood the author expresses far more interesting than the writer's religious or spiritual insight. He's particularly good on the "factual fictions" of Lillian Hellman and Norman Mailer.

16. This short paragraph from John Henry Newman's *Apologia pro Vita Sua: Being a History of His Religious Opinions* (note the "his") (New York: Penguin Classics, 1995) may stand for the kind of conversion "experience" endemic to theological Christian authors. "When I was fifteen, (in the autumn of 1816,) a great change of thought took place in me. I fell under the influences of a definite Creed, and received into my intellect impressions of dogma, which, through God's mercy, have never been effaced or obscured" (25).

17. There is an epic plotline to these books of accursed family faith. Parents, who are members of a charismatic cult, set up an authoritarian, at times torturous, regime their children must follow: all things require scriptural rules. In some of the books, the writer begins to awaken on the narrator's behalf to the indoctrination. Using her wiles—much as slaves in the South once *played* the master—the writer and the narrator connive to free her psychically from the cult, or else she runs for the exit.

18. Leo Tolstoy, *The Death of Ivan Ilyich and Confession*, trans. Peter Carson (New York: Liveright, 2013).

19. Martine de Courcel, *Tolstoy: The Ultimate Reconciliation*, trans. Peter Levi (New York: Charles Scribner's Sons, 1988), 149.

20. Robert Jensen, *Arguing for Our Lives: A User's Guide to Constructive Dialog* (San Francisco: City Lights Books, 2013), 65.

21. Lamott's cascade of Christian memoir begins with her adult conversion in *Traveling Mercies: Some Thoughts on Faith* (Thorndike, ME: Thorndike Press, 1999) and continues with *Plan B: Further Thoughts on Faith* (Thorndike, ME: Thorndike Press, 2005); *Grace (Eventually): Thoughts on Faith* (New York: Riverhead Books, 2007); *Help, Thanks, Wow: The Three Essential Prayers* (New York: Riverhead Books, 2012); *Stitches: A Handbook on Meaning, Hope, and Repair* (New York: Riverhead Books, 2013); *Small Victories: Spotting Improbable Moments of Grace* (New York: Riverhead Books, 2014); *Hallelujah Anyway: Recovering Mercy* (New York: Riverhead Books, 2017); and *Almost Everything: Notes on Hope* (New York: Riverhead Books, 2018). In eight consecutive books, there's a pattern that needs no further explanation. Alternatively, Lamott's best book—deservedly acclaimed—is *Bird by Bird: Some Instructions on Writing and Life* (New York: Anchor Books, 1994), penned before Jesus took the reins.

22. You would think there'd be legions of Christ-loving testaments, especially post-Augustine, between 399 and 1882. Alas, even the knockoffs are members of a tiny club. One of the few in American literature is *The Life and Character of the Late Rev. Mr. Jonathan Edwards*, written in 1740, published in 1765. The lacuna is as abysmal as it is unexamined. Except in Bible movies—of late, we are in a second era of Hollywood's Christianization: *King of Kings* led the way in the 1950s and *The Passion of the Christ* in the 2000s—we almost never meet religious-minded characters in film, literature, or TV serials, HBO's surreal end-times thriller *The Leftovers* notwithstanding.

23. Jill Ker Conway, *When Memory Speaks: Reflections on Autobiography* (New York: Alfred A. Knopf, 1998).

24. *The Portable Medieval Reader*, ed. James Bruce Ross and Mary Martin McLaughlin (New York: Penguin Classics, 1977).

25. Teresa of Avila, *The Life of St. Teresa of Jesus, of the Order of Our Lady of Carmel*, trans. David Lewis, 3rd ed. (London: Thomas Baker, 1904). Available on Project Gutenberg. Quoted in the preface by David Lewis.

26. Ibid., chap. 39, §17.

27. Mary G. Mason "The Other Voice: Autobiographies of Women Writers," in *Women, Autobiography, Theory: A Reader*, ed. Sidonie Smith and Julia Watson, Wisconsin Studies in Autobiography (Madison: University of Wisconsin Press, 1998), 321.

28. Table, "Estimated Illiteracy of Men and Women in England, 1500–1900," from David Mitch, "Education and Skill of the British Labour

Force," in *The Cambridge Economic History of Modern Britain*, ed. Roderick Floud and Paul Johnson, vol. 1, *Industrialisation, 1700–1860* (Cambridge: Cambridge University Press, 2004), 344, reproduced at https://www1 .umassd.edu/ir/resources/laboreducation/literacy.pdf.

29. Thérèse of Lisieux, *The Story of a Soul*, trans. John Clarke (Washington DC: ICS, 1996).

30. Thomas Merton, *The Seven Storey Mountain* (New York: Harcourt, Brace, 1948).

31. Quoted in William H. Shannon, *Thomas Merton: An Introduction* (Cincinnati: St. Anthony Messenger Press, 1997), 132.

32. Thomas Merton, *The Living Bread* (New York: Farrar, Straus and Giroux, 1980), 151.

33. In the Bible, I find it more than curious that the Almighty tells Jacob, "I am the Lord God," expressing a rather large otherness, perhaps the onset of this split personality in literature. (Didn't Richard Nixon assert on occasion, "I am the president!," as if we needed to be reminded of the fact that he actually *was?*)

I note, too, that Jesus utters just once, "When ye have lifted up the Son of man, then shall ye know that I am he." Most of the time his followers regard him as Son. Usually, he's not self-referential but metaphoric: I am "the bread of life," "the light of the world," and "the good shepherd," among other things. It's safe to say that writing has this ability for any of us, gods or mortals, to don a mask: *what we say we are we are*, at least, in our own minds.

And yet, for me, Jesus remains a symbolic, mythical nonindividual, despite so many who buy the reality of his crucifixion. That we should "believe in" him because he died a violent death for humankind's sins, all seventy billion of us who have ever lived. Augustine is a much more authentic model of an actual individual, for he burdens and unburdens himself—a claim as daring as those who portray Jesus divine—as the living embodiment of Christian humanity and Christian suffering. Whatever Christ is, he is not the first Christian: Augustine is.

Finally, why do I say Jesus is a nonindividual? Claims arguing for and against his historical personage will persist forever. I think individuality quantified and qualified by some documentary evidence, the autobiography or memoir (a signed painting or composition would also do), more than makes the case. Augustine's life is authenticated by his writing; Christ's life is hearsay. If I have to "believe in" one over the other, well . . .

34. Roger Lipsey, *Make Peace before the Sun Goes Down: The Long Encounter between Thomas Merton and His Abbot, James Fox* (Berkeley: Shambhala, 2015), 56–57.

35. What might a definition of "spiritual literature" entail? Here's one from a letter by Flannery O'Connor, in 1956, about Simone Weil. "Simone Weil is a mystery that should keep us all humble, and I need it more than most. Also, she's the example of the religious consciousness without a religion which maybe sooner or later I will be able to write about." Flannery O'Connor to "A," December 28, 1956, in *The Habit of Being: Letters of Flannery O'Connor*, ed. Sally Fitzgerald (New York: Farrar, Straus and Giroux, 1979), 189.

Spirituality and
the Memoirist

All writing pretends to be something it's not,
something it can't be.

—*John Edgar Wideman*

The club of Christian autobiographers whose members examine their faith with narrative verve and steely self-awareness
is tiny. Just a handful since Augustine. I'm not sure what to make
of this lacuna. The dearth of such writing is an enigma. Is it the
doubled knot of self- and church-censorship? Is it the cessation of
doubt that religious conversion gives its adherents? Maybe the few
who dig into the psychology of their souls carry some rare chromo-
some, of which the rest of us are barren.

Moreover, despite their literary tenacity—Thérèse's mad cloy-
ing and Merton's sanguine contemplation—today "these books"
are nowhere to be found. Indeed, the absence of a tradition may
have nothing or everything to do with why hundreds of recent

American writers, some of whom were once church-affiliated, are disentangling their spiritual sensibilities. One thing is certain: they are observing themselves less through a religion's lens and more through the writer's longing to experience *as text* the depth of the self.

To explore this notion further, let me unpack what is sometimes called the "spiritual autobiography." My apologies to those antsy with all this overlapping terminology. But I need to recognize John D. Barbour and his essay "Autobiography."[1] Among the questions Barbour asks about combining a spiritual theme with "literary originality" in a writer's oeuvre are these: "Does it make sense to see a work as spiritual when the search for self replaces the desire to know God, and when the goal of defining a unique personal identity becomes more important than otherworldly salvation, adherence to orthodox beliefs, or commitment to a community? Is a book a spiritual autobiography if its author is more concerned with literary originality than with fidelity to a received religious tradition?" (703).

This is one of the sharpest ways to characterize the forms I'm examining: the classic religious autobiographer looks for the incomparable nature of God, while the feisty spiritual memoirist looks for the incomparable nature of the self. The pagan Oracle of Delphi says, Know thyself. In our time, such a prophecy is rapidly replacing Christ's Come unto me.

I think this sudden transference from divinely ordered to individually vested arrived during the 1990s and 2000s. A new generation of scriptors, to use Barthes's term, beheld the Horsemen of the Spiritual Memoir galloping their way. How surprised they were, at the same time, to be galloping away from all-encompassing certitude. It's beyond the scope of this book (someone will traverse the idea one day) to affix the precise historical shift from the redemption-bent life story to the meandering, ahistorical, and self-obsessed inquiry. But a shift from former to latter has occurred. And to understand its strains and themes, to outline some of its causes and effects, guides the remainder of my say.

ぱ

MANY CONTEMPORARY spiritual memoirs are seasoned with liminal insight.[2] These books feature a prime relationship between the author and a place, a family, a lover, or the inner self who longs to be found or is content with being lost. Some of these memoirs dovetail religious concerns and soul matters and occasionally spill over into "inspiration." But more often, the writer marshals a finely plotted narrative to shape how the spiritual seed was planted, has grown, and continues to grow in the prose itself. If that seed is there, intrinsic and immanent, it means the author needs its comfort. In the majority of these books, there's no conversion, no return of a lost childhood faith. The person, as I say, hungers to elope with the spirit, or, better, the spirit steals her away, that is, as long as she trusts the finger-curling come hither. She is homing in on that concrete event or image that has brought about the risky release of a luminous spark.

In one of the most touchingly meditative books ever written, *Gift from the Sea* by Anne Morrow Lindbergh (1955),[3] we find scant mention of God and nothing about religion. But we do feel Lindbergh is being guided by an inner spiritual need, perhaps, from her own agency. Of her hope to find "peace with myself" in the midst of a life oversaturated with fame and terror—the baby she and Charles, her husband, birthed was, at twenty months, taken, held for ransom, and murdered in 1932—she writes:

> I want a singleness of eye, a purity of intention, a central core to my life that will enable me to carry out these obligations and activities as well as I can. I want, in fact—to borrow from the language of the saints—to live "in grace" as much of the time as possible. I am not using this term in a strictly theological sense. By grace I mean an inner harmony, essentially spiritual, which can be translated into outward harmony. I am seeking perhaps what Socrates asked for in the prayer from the *Phaedrus* when he said, "May the outward and inward man be at one." I would like to achieve

> a state of inner spiritual grace from which I could function
> and give as I was meant to in the eye of God. (17)

There's crafted elegance here, plus careful abstraction, so as not to make faith the foible. In a short book, she scours the beach for shells, ocean species, and sea-worn rocks whose wave-tossed materiality resembles her own. Her audience knew that she had been crucified in the media, that the loss of a child stalked her, that she was a talented artist and writer, and that the peace she sought for herself was on top of the duty she bore to a man and his notoriety, which for her, included being the dominant parent of their four (surviving) children. (Lindbergh is circumspect, mentioning neither duty nor dominance nor any of her family.)

Gift from the Sea is a meditation on her disequilibrium. The intimacy is striking, an inner serenity affectingly mirrored for her in Maui. I've always admired this book. Its snail-paced and object-obsessed writing is deeply felt. The things she wants are not God-made per se. They are, what we all want, a calm in the storm: for her, solitude, simplicity, time, and rest before she returns to their Connecticut home and vacuous celebrity. Absent Bible, Christ, church, or afterlife, she steers clear of the credal ramparts that many readers expect and sits beach-calmed with the soulful breakers. The spiritual in her is an ever-emerging natural presence, without face or spine, nothing creaturely, neither more nor less than the timelessness of the ocean, the sand, the rock, the wind. The book feels wholly sui generis, its realms of sea and self effortlessly communing.

Still another feature: Lindbergh's personal style becomes her story. She employs sparse narrative with much description and reflection. Her book contains barely any statements of belief—belief she ascribes to or, for that matter, wants us to ascribe to. What spiritual development looks like in the life of Lucky Lindy's wife is the long, hard slog it takes to probe her interior self and ask what precisely *she* needs to write about. The emphasis is on *her*.

And in that emphasis is a clue about why it's enough for many authors like Lindbergh to compose a seamless book, a short, poignant memoir or a collection of contemplative essays. The book itself is the statement of belief. No, amend that. Not belief exactly. Rather, the confession of its void, without rancor, and, in its place, the balm of nature, even if imagined or therapeutic. Lindbergh accounts for herself many years into her private struggle. She poses questions, hunts for grace, receives it from the sea, and, once tendered, finds that she is renewed, which we feel for her and ourselves, with a clearer sense of what she's always had—her beloved and burdensome longing.

❦

WHEN I say a memoir is spiritual, I also mean it is—and almost has to be—an innovative prose composition. Often, I find in these books the writer as literary activist who uses the ongoingness of narrative nonfiction to spark periodic and abrupt entries into other spheres (bedazzled longer than the shrine tourist) where an unknown force or condition, call it the memoirist's deepest enthrallment, is waiting, ready to realign the teller.

Some context.

In "Conversion and the Language of Autobiography,"[4] Geoffrey Galt Harpham contextualizes the then-current (1988) state of life-writing and religion. First, he says that in the past religious conversion occurs "in dialogue with texts," and in a society "already the product of conversion." Such work reflects "the assurances of a coherent and metaphysically unproblematic existence within an elaborately secured culture, in a preconverted, stable world." In short, an overwhelmingly Christian *Weltansicht*.

Writers like D. H. Lawrence and Langston Hughes did away with that conceit: their "revelations," Harpham continues, "seem the expressions of selves altogether more improvisatory, ad hoc, and provisional than their predecessors." The old autobiographical form, he notes, is "a mode of self-expression that confirms, depicts, and enacts conversion. . . . Our writers are more likely to insist on the failures of conversion" (49). Unpack the implication: failure of conversion is also the failure of "a preconverted, stable world." If the dominant culture is no longer Christian, then both religious conversion and deconversion are states of being without a country.

Harpham goes further. He says that any tale, especially when the claimant has been "saved," is, in part, a fiction because it's "incapable of fully representing, much less transforming, existence." Much remains outside the book: "the life of the body in time, the act of the writing itself, the fact of life after autobiography." These facets "resist transformation, idealization, and narrative closure" (49). Religious authors dispose of uncertainty by pinnacling faith—and its undeniability in their lives—as prima facie evidence. Spiritual writers end as they began, uncertain there's any evidence to speak of. Such may, in turn, absorb another beat of life's meaninglessness.

Here's a familiar plot. We walk into a rushing stream and feel around our ankles three currents. As authorial currents, they are those who (1) narrate their spiritual breakthroughs, (2) reflect on their ineffability, and (3) entangle breakthrough and reflection. Shoes soggy, feet blistered, we find these journeys sprung from hope and hopelessness, common to us all. To write spiritually acts as a change agent in one's life as well as in the inner mutations and deceits writing often enacts. As a result, *a* or *no* sudden entry to the coveted "other" domain occurs.

I balance *an entry* and *no entry* because of two questions engendered from my reading. First, can a spiritual memoir manifest the inexplicable and never find it, that is, enact all trial-and-error and no enlightenment? And second, can a spiritual memoir discover a core ambiguity inherent in spirituality itself, which overturns the faith-based certainty that there is *no* core ambiguity?

I recall Dani Shapiro's closing punt in *Devotion*,[5] her dive into her family's Judaism and her New Age sojourns with Buddhism and mindfulness. She writes, "I was pretty sure there was no parking-spot-procuring God, swooping down from on high, helping out in a crisis—or even a traffic jam. I wished I believed that—but I didn't. I simply didn't" (235). She ends the book half-heartedly, anemically, putting up a mezuzah on her doorway so she'll stop, take a breath, and listen. For what, she's still unsure.

Perhaps the *memoir* is one way (like fasting or a pilgrimage) to summon the inexplicable, to say what's unsayable. The irony is, even though you acknowledge Billy Collins's dictum that poem, essay, and memoir "resist verbal description," you've done your best to resist that dictum as well. Indeed, memoir or personal narrative is the very reason you've sheltered at a silent retreat or walked El Camino de Santiago. And if the journal-keeper conforms to no creed, the act of writing itself may become a sacralizing event. Remember, writing about one's life is as much self-caressing as it is self-altering: the story we tell enacts and entombs experience, raising it and burying it simultaneously.

GETTING OUT of the house, getting out of church, getting out of town, or getting out of the self (any of these will suffice) often provokes writers to confront and express a longing for the numinous. And yet to be drawn to supernal spadework does not label those independent authors I've touched on—Anne Morrow Lindbergh, Billy Collins, Bruce Lawrie, Dani Shapiro, and more to come— religious per se. Indeed, the roads most of them trod contend with Christian hegemony in America, call it faith's "deep state," in play since the Great Awakening two hundred years ago and the putative need for Americans *to be religious, if not Christian.* This one institution has so infiltrated its worldview into our culture, shaped by its European and African holdovers our ideas and images and myths about God and evil, suffering and death, the afterlife and the unknown, that serious memoirists have to guard against the melodrama Christ-consciousness and its dogma have brought.

But note, I say *have brought.* What no longer fits is that a Christian saturation of the culture (in the arts, for sure, perhaps less sure in politics) has all but dried up in our lifetimes.

It's no coincidence that in Annie Dillard's intimate natural history of a riverside chunk of rural Virginia, *Pilgrim at Tinker Creek*

(1974),[6] mention of God is scant; references to a church or a community or a family, dysfunctional or not, as well as musings on sin and lust, are nil. In lieu of such shibboleths are the nonhuman habitats of water, trees, flowers, fields, and earth, in which Dillard gets soiled or wet or naughtily esoteric, practicing her obsessional observation. (Dillard was twenty-nine when the book was published; it won the Pulitzer Prize for nonfiction.) What she activates as subject matter is far more significant than its spiritual amorphousness—and yet none of the holiness for her subject is lost on her: Nature displays "an extravagance of care," which is given by a creator to the "extravagance of minutiae."

Dillard extends the idea of a creator and his/her creation not only into nature but also into the quantification of biological facticity and, eventually, into a companionable metaphysics. Working deductively, Dillard nudges the soul-bearing out of the material (as D. H. Lawrence does), but only after *enough* of the material is named, charted, handed, marveled at, hallucinated over, given symbolic weight to, and so on.

(I am careful not to overemphasize the spiritual side of things since most of *Pilgrim* celebrates, even flaunts, biological fact like a Saks Christmas window. By contrast, her writerly mentor, Henry David Thoreau, harmonizes nature and philosophy equally in his tract *Walden*. Neither writer speaks of a personal God. Moreover, it's the intensely portrayed bric-a-brac—"the scandal of particularity"—through which Dillard's larger evolutionary ideas surface.)

The conceit at the heart of this sustained narrative is not easily inferred. Dillard, a sort of word magician, disinters the multiplicity of creation hiding under river-rolled rocks all around her. By sitting in a spot for hours, she disrobes river-wood-and-field and tracks some one item or else examines layers of particularity in a spoonful or a specimen jar of inert/alive stuff. Home, she wields a microscope or dog-ears one of her naturalists' books.

She ranges into nature no more than a duelist's pace from her front porch. The nearby creeks, Tinker and Carvin, are "an active

mystery, fresh every minute. Theirs is the mystery of the continuous creation and all that providence implies: the uncertainty of
vision, the horror of the fixed, the dissolution of the present, the
intricacy of beauty, the pressure of fecundity, the elusiveness of the
free, and the flawed nature of perfection. The mountains . . . are
a passive mystery, the oldest of all. Theirs is the one simple mystery of creation from nothing, of matter itself, anything at all, the
given" (2–3).

Audible here, in this early pronouncement of the book's
spiritual theme, is the tack of measuring, as opposed to idealiz-
ing, nature's bounty. Dillard admits that the environs she observes
are unstable; their limitlessness is less at issue than the fact that
we cannot see the essence of what is right in front of us. Despite
our binoculars and telescopes, we only contemplate nature's sinu-
ous wholeness. What *is* in our DNA is how, given the tools, *given
the words*, we translate physical things into representational and
metaphysical things, body into soul. The best we can do, the best
Dillard can do, is witness a creek overflowing its banks, "roving
frantically to escape, big and ugly, like a blacksnake caught in a
kitchen drawer" (149).

Note that Dillard's absorbed and absorbing particularity, the
analysis one woman exacts beside a creek in an eastern American
state in the early 1970s, need not be fixed as a religious gateway.
As though her viewpoint reveals the holy or the intended. What it
does reveal, even ceremoniously, is a fount of wonder. Dillard un-
derscores her wonder when she says her "creator" is a force without
judgment or commands or age whose presence is as intrinsic to its
creation as its absence—present in its uncountable, ever-divisible
forms and absent in its leaving in that minutiae no calling card, no
ID, no reason for being other than being.

DILLARD IS the soberest of our spirit-summoning writers. In her
there is little of Pico Iyer's tense spiritual longing or Billy Collins's re-
sistive aesthetic or Thomas Merton's Catholic obsession or Thérèse

of Lisieux's purpled dominion or Bruce Lawrie's waiting on God. At one point, in the chapter "The Present," Dillard muses on our split consciousnesses: the seminal consciousness is "innocence" or "pure devotion," while its antagonist, self-consciousness, a "useless interior babble," interrupts our unfettered awareness of the world. She brands the party-pooper as ego, that which ignites vanity and halts innocence, halts its "inward flames of eternity," makes us embarrassingly conscious of ourselves as agents of ourselves. "It is ironic," she writes, "that the one thing that religions recognize as separating us from our creator—our very self-consciousness—is also the one thing that divides us from our fellow creatures. It was a bitter birthday present from evolution, cutting us off at both ends" (79).

Here, Dillard gives herself too little credibility. Of course, we wake up to our waking up; we "murder to dissect," as Wordsworth so scoldingly put it. However, after *The Prelude*, writers have been bequeathed the perceptual task of seeing their spitting image everywhere in the human and the nonhuman realms. I think this is one of the prime motivations to write memoir today. I don't think for a minute our self-consciousness cuts us off *from* anything. On the contrary. It is primal to our species, this seeing out and into the other so as to see into the other within.

It is the nature of contemporary art to emphasize such personal discovery; moreover, many of us are called, often postmodernly, to ascribe flaws to the apparatus of our consciousness and our memory as a means of verifying their (relative) truthfulness. (David Sedaris, of course, is the exception.) Contemporary arts teach us to be attentive much as meditation shows us that we are the subject and the object of our thoughts. If Dillard was truly vexed by "self-consciousness," then that would have been her point. She would have written, I trust, a very different book.

Mostly, Dillard leaves pristine her envisaging power. That power speaks (writes) for itself. She is, however, not a mere observer. She's an assessor, a bridge, a participant, not a *nature* author, no John James Audubon or Joseph Wood Krutch. Dillard proposes that nothing we see today is changing. We only observe its potential. Instead, she changes. Recognizing the gap, the writer gains agency. Because *she* has written it. It's her take. Indeed, the writing produces the credit and the credit is due.

Here's just one sentence that typifies this approach: "The point of the dragonfly's terrible lip, the giant water bug, birdsong, or the beautiful dazzle and flash of sunlighted minnows, is not that it all fits together like clockwork—for it doesn't, particularly, not even inside the goldfish bowl—but that it all flows so freely wild, like the creek, that it all surges in such a free, fringed tangle" (137).

Of course, there is none of Thérèse's self-entitlement in Dillard's prose. No ping issues from the plucked string of the nun's heavenly harp. Thérèse consecrates herself to an unquenchable longing for the pure Christ, for what can never be material again, while Dillard penetrates that which she touches and smells, sees and hears, things she wastes no words longing for. She esteems— more as devotion than fantasy—the ephemeral struggles she reports on in the everydayness and the seasonality of nature. It is hard for us to accept, as Dillard does, that material life is all there is. That nature is an end in itself. That nature is *nonrepresentational*, principally after a couple centuries in which we've compounded glens and glades and benign creatures with Beethoven's Pastoral Symphony.

Today, memoirists like Dillard are forging an unchurched, ahistorical, and deromanticized relationship between the materiality, perceived and yet to be perceived, of humankind and nature. Surprise or not, we are subject to the same cycles of life and death as nature is. We've been granted no exemption. If we experience a transcendent reality, we do so just as we animate, witness, fight off, deny, run from, and make peace with cycles of creation and destruction in our own lives. Such is the incarnation of Dillard's pilgrim's path.

THE BRAWNY tradition of naturalist writers includes Henry David Thoreau, John Muir, Aldo Leopold, Annie Dillard, and others—each part scientist, part ecocentric, part literary maven, part idealist. These ornery sorts compose a polemical (often the men) but also a sentient (often the women) memoir, in avid closeness with and inevitable self-deportation from nature. The closeness is obvious; the opposition happens when each realizes he or she is forever a tourist among the pines; coming back, they must, to be worthy, tell the tale of their elopement and their return to civilization. Thoreau, in *Walden, or, Life in the Woods* (1854), approaches nature with a personal and social morality, the two almost indistinguishable; he imagines a society modeled on eco-preservation, voluntary poverty, and decentralized living—an agrarian utopia, which is impossible and antithetical to the colonizing need of human communities, especially American expansionism. It takes a few generations of American writers to reengage nature as a place of human/other intention—for ethical, conservationist, and private ends. Today, these scribes number in the thousands, albeit with one slightly mad subgroup whose passion to redeem themselves must occur outside.[7]

Take Cheryl Strayed's *Wild: From Lost to Found on the Pacific Crest Trail* (2012).[8] Her tale is significant for many reasons but chiefly because it is a woman's *solo* trek and because the trek itself allows her the space, time, and landscape to grieve her piled-up hardships: marriage infidelity, divorce, a mother who died, a raggedy dispersed family, and the author's unsorted chaos—her randy sexuality, her heroin-supplying boyfriend, and her drug dependency. These ostensible prerequisites for the contemporary woman who writes a memoir to free herself from her excesses is, with Strayed, grippingly readable. Her eleven-hundred-mile walk (almost half the Mexico-to-Canada length) is alive with naïve recklessness and squeamish decisioning.

Almost everything is a surprise, and these subsume her during the three-month, hopscotching sojourn. These things are consistently conflictual, rocking in opposition throughout. They include: Strayed's periods of aloneness and encounters with other hikers (though she walks mostly on her own, the largest portion of the book is given to human interactions, almost all entirely benign);

her ill-preparation for the trek (the image/fact of her boots a size too small is perfect) and her canny, willful adaptations; her need to pay attention to the wilderness's dangers and the sudden reveries she gets lost in, causing Strayed to lose her focus (call it losing focus in order to gain focus); her acclimatizing to, among other trials, searing foot pain the first two weeks (a time frame that accounts for a third of the book); her breezy freestyle gamboling through Oregon later on; and her longing to return to some sense of security amid the constant and more numerous food fantasies she indulges as she trudges along, mile after mile of "trail magic."

Does *Wild* possess a spiritual dimension? Oddly, yes.

On the surface, it seems, she avoids matters of the soul, so busy is she with the hike's planning, camping, sleeping, wounding, bandaging, and keeping on. Who has time to reflect or to fashion coherency out of startling run-ins with rattlesnakes, bears, ice fields, cliff falls, hunger, thirst, deviant men, and ungrieved memories? What's clear is that Strayed is a None. She neither believes in God nor has any faith allegiance to battle (or return to). She does, though, pray to God when her mother is stricken with lung cancer. (God's unresponsiveness ends when Strayed calls him/her "a ruthless bitch.") The beauty of *Wild* is that she is disarmingly free from nearly all credal systems, except making it through each stumble-prone day, which allows her to pursue her own best interest, animating, moment by moment, the tiger woman who must endure.

She does, however, seek a kind of redemption, perhaps unwittingly, via ankle-twisting agony. Early on, she states that she made the "unreasonable decision to take a long walk alone on the PCT in order to save myself" (5). From what, at first, we're not sure. Perhaps a heroin overdose, perhaps the blossoming despair that riddles her after her mother, the closest person in her life, has died. (Actually, Mom died four years prior, but Strayed can't move on, it's clear, until she lives the loss, which is both the hike and documenting it.) Walking north into higher elevations, she finds the time and the space where the composing writer can reflect on the journey but also assess who she wants to be while *being it*, assess what, if anything, she wants to imagine, to personally test and, eventually, espouse. (The espousal is, of course, the memoir itself.) It isn't long before a salvational intent is clear. Whether she's forecasting or has reached it, Strayed is aware, under a sea of stars, that "something growing" in her is "strong and real." Once her youth "became unmoored by sorrow," she notes, that strong and real sensibility is the "thing that would make me believe that hiking the Pacific Crest Trail was my way back to the person I used to be" (17). Such personhood she collects as her love affairs, her long-gone innocence, her girlhood with horses, all of which we get in spades for the rest of the trek.

The person I used to be. This longing is one of the mystical traits of spiritual memoir, time-bending or time-leaping. How curious that the past person is still growing in her. Or is she backpedaling to the strength of character she once had? This uncovering of her core self will not be denied—by loss, by trail, by fear, certainly not by any creator's design. In its own leaps across time, memoir merges past and present selves. What's more, flipping Lyotard's reflections on Augustine, the person she is not yet is the person she was. The *not yet* is the person from the past she hopes to be again and may, in fact, become. Such becoming drives the narrative.

It's not always the future of the writer which is at stake in the spiritual memoir. Rather, it is the earlier-in-life wholeness that each of us has and knows is uncoverable, that authentic *once-was* to whom we make pilgrimage, one who neither then nor now follows any religious byway. Indeed, Strayed's path, utterly guileless, leaps over all faith paths because its jungle clearings and totemic goals (the book has sold millions) are common yens, especially for women.

WELCOME TO a world in which self-reliance is center stage, despite the money and supplies Strayed receives at mail stops every couple of weeks. Self-reliance is as much will as luck, as much learned skill repurposed as canny diversion. Still, none escapes the dread and the sublimity of the Mojave and the Sierra.

And yet Strayed, in her briefly captured reflections, grasps that this trek is not the greatest adversary of her life. The toughest foe is her mother's death, which, ironically, is what "made me believe the most deeply in my safety: nothing bad could happen to me, I thought. The worst thing already had" (59). Thus, the pile of past and present things, tormenting and exhausting her, is incessantly being placed by the hiker-writer into perspective. For me, it's the muscular strength of this tale. Strayed ever coming out of peril and ad-libbed adjustment and ever going into safety and roused calm. Rinse and reverse and repeat. No different from the path itself. (The path just leads to more path, its unending destination.) One day, she clambers a few miles and the blisters and dwindling water become unbearable, while another day (later and seasoned), she glides nineteen miles in monkish serenity, the blackened toenails, the ankle cuts, the hip bruises, the muscle fatigue all fallen by the wayside, albeit temporarily.

Strayed produces way more narrative drama and way less analytic gloss; the scenic routine, in a leisurely sensory pace, thickens the foresty prose. The day-to-day instances are packed like fat cells: she is blithely recalling a pop song from the 1970s and then trips on a rock, falls, and gashes her knee. How curious that the tonnage (call it the *load*) is her trudging and dallying, getting depressed, getting psyched, the mind, the handmaid of the body, electrified by desire and fear, in its depressed or manic state. These extremes bump into each other constantly, which spells much of the soloist's drama, cinematically represented and far outside the unencumbered lives many of us fumble through in the urban jungle.

What emerges out of this quotidian flint, sticks rubbed together, is a belly full of fire, a spelunker's torch, a candle in the uncursed dark. Here is one lamplit moment right after she nicknames her backpack Monster.

> I was amazed that what I needed to survive could be carried
> on my back. And, most surprising of all, that I could carry it.
> That I could bear the unbearable. These realizations about
> my physical, material life couldn't help but spill over into
> the emotional and spiritual realm. That my complicated life
> could be made so simple was astounding. . . . By the end of
> that second week, I realized that since I'd begun my hike, I
> hadn't shed a single tear. (92)

What we are hearing—and it happens in inverse proportion to
the sheer amount of hiking Strayed describes—is the writer, at last,
waking up. It has taken time, but the walker, still asleep in her past,
has begun opening her eyes and seeing what's in front of her. Little
else for me speaks of the spiritual dimension more strongly than
these isolated moments of Strayed cracking awake. Such cracks, as
Leonard Cohen sings, are how the light gets in.

Here it doesn't matter whether the fissure comes *on* the hike
or *in* the writing. I doubt she's noting down her "later" reflections
"during" the journal-keeping she did on the trail. Walking the
PCT and recording it require sizable endurances, which, for me,
verify the walk *and* the words as necessary to each other.

In the wilderness, such cracks are common, though Strayed,
preferring judiciousness, is careful not to overtend them. Still, she
is attuned (the Sierra Nevada has attuned her) to *suddenness*, its
dangers and its joys, a territory most of us never occupy. Suddenness kept the senses of Native Americans on alert. The nomadic
tribes were constantly enlivened by ample potable water, by the
bee-loud quiet, by the telltale smell of other dwellers, human and
animal. Tribes were also decimated by disease, accident, drought,
and conquest. Amid it all, the idea of sudden beauty, of insight,
flourished; the result was a heightened inspiriting of life, captivat-
ing everyone with even greater wildness.

The knife of human consciousness sharpens our sensibilities
when our immediate survival is at stake. We face an extreme
circumstance—say, when Strayed backtracks twenty miles, the

trail lost—and she must become her own agent. We enlarge in equal measure to the hills and valleys we traverse. We find a symbiosis, set DNA-deep, where material and spiritual domains are still fused. Hikers call this becoming one with the mountain.

TAMING NATURE is not Cheryl Strayed's writerly trophy. Instead, it's drawing out and taking in the means by which nature—the great unknown—reshapes her, which is, no surprise, what the trail is *for*. Sounds spiritual—to be restored by nature, the hobbling self a hardened corpsman. If this is so, do we then call any memoir with extinct volcanoes and miles of Douglas fir as context spiritually redeeming?

It's not just the author's troubled youth that ushers in salvation. To be saved requires a *there*, an explorable, survivable locale where spirit reigns. Call such places those that challenge the intruder because the intruder, in desperation, has lost or misplaced or never had what suffused our ancestors: a paradisal world at their fingertips, which is still available in the western deserts and mountain ranges of the United States.

What is this burden of place in the context of our culture? Into Strayed's glory-bound hike, there are, whether she's conscious of it or not, echoes of the cliché, American exceptionalism. You stake your claim, pan the river, outlast torrential rains and prospector's greed, and yelp when you chance onto the gold nugget, the reward of your stick-to-itiveness. Here, I'm mindful again of *Walden*. In it, Thoreau, communing with ponds and forests, rapacious bugs and New England winters, revivifies that which civilization depletes and which only nature restores. What's restored is the spirit (Americans, who avoid the outdoors, are ever "spiritually impoverished"), arriving for the solitary soul at water's edge or on mountain ridge. The idea that nature is a fount for the soul revives our romance with nativism: Native American and America First! are both in play. But we seldom speak of this as a community, as the "church of the wild," a coinage we should circumvent.

Still, the call is to go rogue and, like Strayed, become "a majority of one"—Thoreau's self-crowning and self-crowing phrase from "Civil Disobedience."

To write spiritually one must try the never tried, welcome danger, exit one's zone. Adventure for the spiritual memoirist has to come with *intent*. Strayed is what I call an intentional memoirist, facing that which few of us choose. She heads out toward an ill-prepared goal but a goal nonetheless—to corral her own agency by butting up against nature's agency. Six-mile-wide and nineteen-hundred-feet-deep Crater Lake, in southern Oregon, "remained inexplicable," she writes. "The Klamath tribe still considered the lake a sacred site and I could see why. I wasn't a skeptic about this." No, she's convinced, what with the searing pain in her feet. "I could feel the lake's power. It seemed a shock in the midst of this great land: inviolable, separate and alone, as if it had always been and would always be here" (272).

Immortal, yes, though its intentional nature will always be hidden.

WHEN WRITERS (attempt to) balance their dominion with nature's, they bypass the whims of a judgmental God and confront the whims of an even fickler realm—that of do-or-die survival in the starkest of climes. The most beautiful of such exhaustive and foreign journeys is *The Snow Leopard* (1978) by Peter Matthiessen.[9] The book's literary pleasures, alas, are too many to enumerate here. But I'd wager that the greatest of these pleasures is how well Matthiessen, at the time a student of Zen Buddhism, relegates his spiritual experience to a subordinate role, even though the trek into the sublime Nepalese Himalaya of the Tibetan Plateau guarantees him majestic moments of enlightenment. To exaggerate these moments is the *ne plus ultra* of Christian confession—of all confessional tracts—even the scrupulously spiritual memoir.

Like Strayed, Matthiessen focuses largely on that which is not "I." In a simple ratio, his concentration on geography, native inhabitants, culture, regional history, animals, ecology, Buddhism, and the tortuous climb to the Crystal Monastery in northwest Nepal equals 80 percent, his inner journey, 20. Place, culture, history, and hike rule. Reflective self-regard retreats when place, culture, history, and hike are massively *on*. (Apologies to the New Agers: There is no self-improvement to be had in this book.) For the writer to make any Zen sense of what lies before him, the space/time context has to be there: participating in, and meditating on, the facts of life. "Though I am blind to it," Matthiessen writes, "the Truth is near, in the reality of what I sit on—rocks." Still, we *can't help but* notice the Western person, the "I," perceiving the importance of all this, in part because he is among the first, an Odysseus who ventures out and returns with the tale. We note the stamp on the seer: the man is, ironically, more amplified because the frontier he passes through awakens him to the limitations of the person who is awakening. Before I argue that such a turn is significant for this soul explorer, a brief background on the book.

Matthiessen's memoir is both a real-time diary and worked-over journal about his and zoologist George Schaller's journey to the Land of Dolpo, a mountainous region, between 13,000 and 18,000 feet, dotted with a few plants, animals, and ethnic Tibetans. The trek lasts from September 28 to December 1, 1973.[10] Schaller (GS) and Matthiessen, who is Schaller's guest, walk two hundred miles with Sherpas, who tote supplies and make camps. Schaller is studying the bharal or blue sheep's migration, while Matthiessen hopes to locate the sheep's predator, the snow leopard. A devotee of Zen and its Himalaya origins, the author tracks ascent and descent and then broadens the tale into existential inquiry—"individual existence, ego, the 'reality' of matter and phenomena are no more than fleeting and illusory arrangements of molecules" (86)—or narrows it, for example, onto the Tarakots, a group of native guides, who "hunch like growths among the snow patches, wrapped in old blankets, doing nothing at all to better their condition, despite the prospect of a long night of bitter cold"; they "have carried no firewood, and must scavenge rice from us, and most are barefoot" (95).

As noted, the roped bundle of the tale is its bricolage of facts; only occasionally does Matthiessen surprise himself with intuitions while this goatish terrain reattunes his being. The book's quantitative emphasis lies in his explaining his observations, as much scientist as explorer. Matthiessen's rapture is both near and far, bursting forth when the spirit of place jolts him. What makes *The Snow Leopard* so pleasurable is that we get a lapidary portrait of Nepal infused, like diamonds cut to accent their luminosity, with bits of spine-straightening awe.

First, an example of the Matthiessen fact. (The book contains an index, naming people, sites, concepts, and more.) Midjourney, one evening he and GS make camp.

> Having pitched our tents again, we set off up the steep mountain, which has open grass on these lower slopes due to south exposure. Soon a hill fox appears, intent upon its hunting, ignoring us, it makes six pounces in eight minutes, four of them successful, though its game is small. One victim is a mouse—mouse holes and snow tunnels, exposed by thaw, are everywhere around our feet—and two more, seen through the spotting scope, look like big grasshoppers, and the fourth is a long thin gleam of life that is perplexing. Later, when the sun is high, I find some shiny striped gray skinks that solve the mystery. Despite the unseasonal blizzards of the late monsoon, this midautumn mountainside is still alive, and the seeds and myriad insects stuck to the snow patches attract the migrant redstarts as well as large mixed flocks of pipits, larks, rose finches, and the like. Dwarf rhododendron, edelweiss, blue gentian occur sparsely, and above 15,000 feet, wherever stone protrudes, bright lichens of all colors deck the snow. The white is patterned by the pretty tracks of snow cock, blue sheep, fox, and smaller creatures: we look in vain for the pug marks of snow leopard. And soon we drift apart like grazing animals, in silence, as we do almost every day along the trail. GS pursues three

blue sheep that move diagonally up the slope, while I climb
to the base of a huge rock pile on the sky. (97–98)

Second, an instance of Matthiessen's pith. When they arrive
at the frozen monastery, he climbs one morning to a "wind shelter"
where he watches the birds. If there's a snow leopard about, it will
linger for a few days after a sheep kill. Birds will give it away.

> I grow into these mountains like a moss. I am bewitched.
> The blinding snow peaks and the clarion air, the sound
> of earth and heaven in the silence, the requiem birds, the
> mythic beasts, the flags, great horns, and old carved stones,
> the rough-hewn Tartars in their braids and homespun boots,
> the silver ice in the black river, the Kang, the Crystal Moun-
> tain. Also, I love the common miracles—the murmur of
> my friends at evening, the clay fires of smudgy juniper, the
> coarse dull food, the hardship and simplicity, the content-
> ment of doing one thing at a time: when I take my blue tin
> cup into my hand, that is all I do. We have had no news
> of modern times since late September, and will have none
> until December, and gradually my mind has cleared itself,
> and wind and sun pour through my head, as through a bell.
> Though we talk little here, I am never lonely; I am returned
> into myself. (228)

Matthiessen has a method. Using the present tense, he writes
mostly in durational time, merging, day by day, step by step, his
quotidian pace with the gargantuan Himalayan domain. This
diurnal constancy energizes him. This is a classic travel diary; he
records more *of*—and reflects less *on*—the inches made, although
the later, off-the-mountain reflector did, no doubt, add shape and
sagacity to the telling.

ANOTHER DAY, Matthiessen is climbing to seventeen thousand
feet, where, "windless and hot," plying "knee-deep snow," he is "in

desperate need of air, floundering," carrying "in a broken basket" "sixty pounds of lentils." Mid-travail, the moment organizes a layered summary and a time-leaping flash:

> As the slopes steepen, I am almost on all fours, knuckles brushing the snow, and this simian stance shifts the weight forward, saving my lacerated shoulders. Three thoughts carry me ahead; the prospect of the northward view over Dolpo to Tibet; the prospect of a free descent across these brilliant snowfields to hot tea and biscuits; and the perception—at this altitude, extremely moving—that these two hands I see before me in the sun, bracing the basket straps, hands square and brown and wrinkled with the scars of life, are no different from the old hands of my father. Simultaneously, I am myself, the child I was, the old man I will be. (167)

This suddenly settling paragraph, one of fourteen in the "October 29" chapter, belies an emotional complexity which, over the chapter's entirety, is a superlative rendering of the man's spirituality. How so?

Two major streams run through "October 29": the stress of near-airless hiking, moving supplies in a topography almost unfit for human traversal, and his shifting between ungrieved memories and trail fears as he grapples with the terrain. A few other details need mentioning. Schaller has sent him word that since he, Schaller, has made it to the monastery, Matthiessen will have to keep hauling food and equipment with the Sherpa guides. Those guides, Matthiessen insists, are finicky and bumbling, not the best supply carriers. Add in a soundtrack: "from somewhere" he hears "the rumble of an avalanche" (166).

Matthiessen is not *at* his destination, the Crystal Mountain / Shey Monastery; he is floundering trying to get there. Waking in the midst of life to the realization that one is inescapably in the midst of life is a touchstone of Zen. Such koan-like insights Matthiessen is experiencing more and more as a novice. By 1981 he'll become, via stepwise study, a Zen teacher, priest, and master. He is realizing that he's emotion-plagued at the same time he doesn't want to be emotion-plagued. A fine way / no-way paradox. Better said, his memories and his nitpicking them, like lice, lessen his participation in the present.

His swirling regrets and fears, however, are the soul of the chapter. Matthiessen narrates how he moves from feeling "open, clear, and childlike" to tears of rage at his wife's death the year before; to laughter at the thought of her scoffing at him, "wailing with lost love" (165); to dizziness as he lurches under the basket's straps; to carping that he's been left this duty unfairly; to a light-bulb moment of timelessness, realizing that his hands are no different from those of his father: "Simultaneously, I am myself, the child I was, the old man I will be" (167); to dreading one slip and fall into the impassivity of this mountainous emptiness; and, finally, to running downhill at sunset to make camp and "wait out the night" (168).

Only at one or two points, reporting on the day's travail, is Matthiessen fully present. Which, considering the circumstances, is pretty good. But studying the chapter, I feel it is the book's most disquieting passage. The day wobbles between his destabilizing emotions (the isolation he's boxed in with goes unresolved for two more chapters) and his rapprochement with the rock-ribbed desolation of Dolpo. Of course, there are good and bad drops into abysmal thought. But this tête-à-tête with the abyss is more than trying; it's a crisis. Caution: this is not Matthiessen's moment of disentangled peace. Just the opposite. This is the mortal coil of our man in Nepal, in part because he is so high-strung and put-upon and pinned in an environment, which, if it sees him at all, is as mere carrion.

In the chapter's third-to-last paragraph, Matthiessen, "confronted with this emptiness," imagines there is a beating heart to the imperturbable void of the planet. Its most commanding silence resides in the Himalaya. That silence drew Lao-tzu, who brought the *Tao Te Ching* to Nepal from China in the sixth century BCE, and that silence pushed out Bodhidharma, who carried Buddhism from India to China a millennium later. Both men at the end of their lives reentered Nepal and "vanished . . . into such emptiness." Like those sages, Matthiessen has come all this way hoping nothingness will welcome him. But alas: "What I see in this first impression is a chaos of bright spires, utterly lifeless, without smoke or track or hut or passing bird" (168).

It's the opposite, too, of contentment. There's a fissure. As a Vedantist philosopher says, "the seen cannot be the seer."[11] The void is without "I" or me or the world arranging itself around me: to reckon existence contains me in any significant way is not the case. As with the medieval mystics, the self is obliterated.

At times, these visions bring Matthiessen stability and peace; at other times, seeing-into-things renders him agape, feeling the wonder of stone or stoned wonder. All perception, no self. But then, whether in his notebook each night in camp or later at his home in Long Island, the act of writing merely shadows the thing itself. Later in the book, Matthiessen remarks: "I understand all this, . . . knowing that mere words will remain when I read it all again, another day" (208). Think of the spiritual not as the tennis court and the net and the players and their rackets but as the ball, always moving, always gamed.

Like that ball, Matthiessen traverses the leopard's backyard, seemingly coming closer, while the leopard is seemingly moving away from detection. The *seeming* is his projection about the Big Cat. Such is the finicky nature of a goal whose rules of engagement are unknowable. Not only is the leopard never seen by Matthiessen, but his desire for the leopard (unlike Ahab's for Moby-Dick) beckons it no nearer. The other thing beckoning him is that he expects the Himalaya trial will release and resolve the nagging grief he carries for his dead wife, Deborah Love.

THIS ILLUSION that keeps Matthiessen from—as well as entices him toward—the leopard backstops the most fraught theme in the book: the persistence of Deborah's memory. Matthiessen and Love, whom he calls "D," were married in 1963. Her interest in Buddhism awakened his. Exiting the sixties' hallucinogenic days, they devoted themselves to Zen study and took vows. By the time Love fell ill with cancer in 1972, the pair, who had a child, Alex (eight years old in 1973), were nearing separation. Marriage, son, a split, and her death lengthen his stride. Though he starts off as a tabula rasa, a novice mountaineer, we come to see how haunted he is.

Shafts of sunlight, the Deborah/Alex story breaks in through-out. Early in the book, Matthiessen quotes from a letter Alex wrote to him before the trek began. The boy tearfully describes how he'll miss his father and signs it, "Your sun." Recalling the day Alex and father said goodbye in early September, Matthiessen noticed birds flying by and butterflies flitting, the presence of rose bushes, and himself unresponsive to his son's sadness. This is the journey: past raised, *keep walking.*

Next, he thinks of Alex's boyish innocence, "still in unison with the primordial nature of creation" (39). This reminds him that the Zen lesson of becoming "one with whatever one does" should buffer loss. Let the missing go, the Buddhists insist. But who does that? Past disputed, *keep walking.*

He remembers meeting Deborah, with whom he shared a de-sire to suss out their "own 'true nature.'" To facilitate the search, they consumed psychedelics. Recklessly. Deborah had worse trips than Peter, but, coming down, they united: "as we held each other, both bodies turned into sapling trees that flowed into each other, grew together in one strong trunk that pushed a taproot deeper and deeper into the ground" (43). Unable to make chemical visions conform to daily life, they abandoned LSD, realizing that drugs made an unwanted "separation of the 'I' from true experience of the One" (44). Husband and wife embraced Zen fully, welcomed its koans. Past flared, *keep walking.*

Suddenly, Matthiessen has a nightmare: Alex is a caged fox, "uncared for, and covered with grime" (55). The author's stricken, and this brings up trouble with Deborah: "To live with a saint is not difficult, for a saint makes no comparisons, but saintlike aspiration presents problems" (73). They quarreled and "the marriage came apart." But Matthiessen stayed with her, and her cancer spread. Past intensified, *keep walking*.

Halfway into the Himalayan journey, Matthiessen treasures an insight he had while Love was dying: He says that "[I] gave myself up to delighted immersion in this Presence, to a peaceful *belonging* so overwhelming that tears of relief poured from my eyes, so overwhelming that even now . . . the memory affects me as I write" (101–2). Past/present fused—a Oneness—*keep walking*.

That insight was, for Matthiessen, the "greatest blessing of my life." Love spoke similarly; her dying, she said, was "one of the happiest times in all my life" (102). Past spiritualized, *keep walking*.

And yet Matthiessen's anxiety continues: On the day Love died, his ego, he writes, dissolved. Was he responsible or was it another agent, a mystical entity? Is this indecisiveness his "True Nature"? Not exactly. It's something else. While he is grateful that "the specter of remorse" has not overtaken him, he is less restive with her death. Yet such a change is one of many "mere tantalizing glimpses" into the multiplex of the self's true nature—when the fog lifts. Present tempted, *keep walking*.

"Still I sit a little while," Matthiessen writes, "watching the light rise to the peaks. In the boulder at my back, there is a shudder, so slight that at another time it might have gone unnoticed. The tremor comes again; the earth is nudging me. And still I do not see" (104). Present arrives, *keep walking*.

Until a ping awakens the book's end when Matthiessen takes another turn on Love's death, writing, "a little after midnight, effortlessly, D died," the moment he and their Zen master held her hands, and "everything was as it should be," and "all was calm and clear." As a remembrance balm, he cites a line from Love's memoir, *Annaghkeen*, about their season of shared passion, living in Ireland: "To proceed as though you know nothing, not even your age, nor sex, nor how you look" (281). Past assuaged, *keep walking*.

And though Matthiessen keeps walking, surprise, not much adds up, not even a synopsis that echoes my clocking of the text's past/present merger. On the one hand, there are twinges of high-mindedness: "With the past evaporated, the future pointless, and all expectation worn away, I begin to experience that *now* that is spoken of by the great teachers" (295). On the other hand, there is the piled-up ongoingness, a knot in the psychic stomach, that won't let him be.

> Now I am spent. The path I followed breathlessly has faded among stones; in spiritual ambition, I have neglected my children and done myself harm, and there is no way back. Nor has anything changed; I am still beset by the same old lusts and ego and emotions, the endless nagging details and irritations—that aching gap between what I know and what I am. I have lost the flow of things and gone awry, sticking out from the unwinding spiral of my life like a bent spring. For all the exhilaration, splendor, and "success" of the journey to the Crystal Mountain, a great chance has been missed and I have failed. I will perform the motions of parenthood, my work, my friendships, my Zen practice, but all hopes, acts, and travels have been blighted. I look forward to nothing. (293)

I DON'T think *The Snow Leopard* is a tale of one man's psychic repair of the past via a "healing itinerary." Rather, it records one in a series of life's intensities rendered meaningful in the writer's post-sojourn self-examination. We know the death of Matthiessen's wife and his son's abandonment have happened; he takes them with him. The trek provides some respite but more adventure until, traipsing down the mountain, he realizes that the heartaches he brought along have persisted. And they are *not* resolved.

Here is the Zen path of this book, one which promises liberation from our dependencies. His Zenish way is nonreligious, raises no specter of Christian determinism. There is no mention of God. There is no Yellow Brick Road to follow. There are no theological weights in his knapsack to unload. There is no wiser Peter Matthiessen coming down off the mountain. As readers, we witness how filled he has been, scraping by, high and low, across the Nepalese Himalaya. Still, we are mistaken if we see this as redemptive. Neither the trek nor *The Snow Leopard* as its record supports such a scheme.

I also note that Matthiessen uses the phrase "spiritual ambition" with disparagement. Why? We imagine we set our gritty lives aside to front-and-center a soul-seeking path. But the demands of food, shelter, sleep, companionship, and shitting intrude no matter what calling we bend to. Matthiessen walks a long time, feet and heart squarely in Zen Buddhist traditions, and he shapes a memoir that refuses (or at least argues with) customary enlightenment.

To write about the path one's personality has insisted one take is Matthiessen's route. Circumlocutionary, I know, but the intent is clear. It's not an exchange, a *this for that*, a trek through the Himalayas as the means to stitch a bleeding wound. Again, why? Because priests and gurus have made it sound as though these are journeys God or the archetype wants us to take. Of course, we can be freed from social constraints, false beliefs, abracadabra. But a quest guarantees no liberation. We still suffer, we still wake up worried. Liberation is the sales pitch of many a religiously or spiritually "inspired" book. Must there be models and morals? Hardly. It's enough just to harness deep feeling and let it bleed or be.

Living seldom frees us from our intrinsic fate (birth family, personality, marriage, parenting), and rarely frees us from our hang-ups, one of which is to keep walking while stuff keeps happening, reasonless, outside the Gates of Eden.

THE MORE I read spiritual authors, the more I see that if the thread gets snagged, it snags on the redemption clause—a man who has earned his salvation and humbly presents that man to the reader.

Matthiessen counters this idea more strongly than anyone I've read. As I've said, he ends the book questioning his motivations and declaring himself a failure. Such is the "moral," such is the "redemption." Along the way, the Buddhist lore he describes does not sentence him to be either a Buddhist or a "better" person. He already is the person he will become. Zen 101. Not that you follow the fourfold path of the Buddha but that you, like him, find your own way. Going it alone doesn't mean Matthiessen got the East wrong; it's that he got himself right. While the trek may lack a lasting purpose or an all-encompassing virtue, it does have intrinsic value as sense-awakening experience. Does his sense-awakening entail transcendent meaning? Perhaps. But it doesn't have to. It demonstrates that the slipperiness of meaning, which Wittgenstein celebrated, is the meaning.[12]

Zen, a philosophy, highlights a stone-cold fact: Most days are like most days. Temporary, fleeting, another link in the chain. But we, the unsettled, deny that the quotidian is enough. We itch, we scratch. We want the thrill of the chase. We hunt for gold doubloons, expecting psychic riches. Whatever it is we want, we think the old Route 66 leads us there. How easily we suppose the spirit sought is the spirit won. It stands to reason that for Matthiessen, who finds unbridled spectacle, the raw outvying the cooked, on his Nepalese journey, there's more to it than just the trek. Why, he ponders in the end, are we disappointed in ourselves during or after we travel among mountains and rivers and through the endangered reaches of the planet, watched over by spectacles of unfeeling grace? Why is the self still deficient?

When we fail, we fail our expectations. Failing our expectations means we gain the accidental, the unwarranted, the impartial. I realize people find value in these things. (If you're a nonfictionist and you cross your spiritual expectation with your certainty that Americans are exceptional, then you're really spending beyond your means.) But, in Matthiessen's portrayal, the sublime flames out and we are left with little to show for it, only the arid emotions of loneliness, chagrin, waste.

To be liberated is to be liberated from failed expectation. Do we then suppose, postadventure, nothing awaits our Odyssean return? Do we then, as Thich Nhat Hanh says, breathe back in to present moment, perfect moment? Why does the question always devolve to *And so, how should I systematize and sell this to others?* No fiction or nonfiction writer I know expects to pen/type/compute a literary how-to. There is no expectation in that department, so there's no failure. There's only the *relative* failure or success of a subjective attempt. For some reason, the idea that texts provide solutions to life's blows is publishing flapdoodle. What makes religious writing religious is its pumping up our inadequacies so we/they need to be ministered to. And what becomes the consequence of that ministering is that the need is unassuageable.

SO: WE arrive at the writer who finds herself adrift, her beliefs challenged, her convictions lost. Such a tale is as ambivalent as it is painful. To salvage what's worthwhile from one's lost religious identity is germane to *Leaving Church: A Memoir of Faith* (2007), by Barbara Brown Taylor, a former Episcopal priest.[13] Listen to the spiritual dryness she voices in her introduction. "I guess you could say that my losses have been chiefly in the area of faith, and specifically in the area of being certain who God is, what God wants of me, and what it means to be Christian in a world where religion often seems to do more harm than good" (xii).

It was not ever thus. Taylor begins the memoir by describing a soulful experience she had at age four. Lying in a field of grass behind her parents' home in Kansas, she feels held, "whether I am pressing down on the earth or the earth is pressing up on me" (22). She feels equally secure when her father buoys her in a swimming pool, teaching her to float. This solidity of support she calls "Presence." "The Presence was not outside me," she writes. "I lived inside the Presence" (25). It's noteworthy that the child's sensibility is shaped by nature—where there is no sin, vengeance, or crucifixion, no ordained judgment.

When the Presence she attests to is gathered up by religion, she becomes not just its participant, but its devotee. Soon the child is churched and, many years on, goes to college, where she eventually earns her PhD at Yale Divinity School. In the late 1980s, she is ordained as an Episcopal priest. The ordination features a laying on of hands, transferring the "Holy Spirit" from the clergy to the newcomer.

While Taylor accedes to the ritual, she has the creepy sense that it's all a performance. They're conferring on her a receptivity to faith that she has in abundance but that also is tied to heavy ecclesiastical responsibility, an apron full of stones. Taking her holy orders, she writes, *"Please, please, please,* I prayed, while the entire weight of heaven and earth pressed down on my head. I was getting exactly what I wanted, but I had not realized how much it was going to hurt" (43).

Next, she "is called" to a church and congregation in a small northeast Georgia mountain town. There she throws herself into service—the pastor who loves too much. She does it all for Grace-Calvary Church—sermons, finances, altar maintenance, officiating at baptisms and weddings and funerals, visiting the sick, counseling the lost and suicidal as well as the petty and the snobbish, composting food, and helping the homeless who sleep in nearby bushes—a mother to hundreds. At one point, she is home when a church worker calls her to say that a woman in the bathroom needs toilet paper; Taylor jumps in her car and delivers a roll. As a priest, she feels "useful to God." She adores "tending the Divine Presence in others." She realizes "why I had been born. To help lift a burden, to help light a path, to help heal a hurt, to help seek a truth" (47). You hear in the "help" phrases her tilting under the conventional duty rectors shoulder. You also hear her lose track of the child's sensation of the holy.

Half of *Leaving Church* is devoted to "Finding," a five-year span (1992–97) in which she is rooted in a place she increasingly wants out of. I am, of course, glossing over what is one of the best pastor immersion stories ever written, not only for its capaciousness but also for its honesty. Taylor loves her flock, of course, but she also dislikes many of the needy little lambs. More vexing is how few parishioners want what's essential to her: worship. Instead, they come to Grace-Calvary to play bingo, comfort themselves with raffles and bake sales, cultivate niceness and sameness. While Taylor's turning away seems gradual, it happens before we know it—a tribute to her ability to steep readers in the slow withering of her commitment until she realizes she's had enough. The honesty that made her so committed to the church, ironically, is the same honesty that issues reasons aplenty to leave.

"Above all," she writes, "I saw that my desire to draw as near to God as I could had backfired on me somehow. Drawn to care for hurt things, I had ended up with compassion fatigue. Drawn to a life of servanthood, I had ended up a service provider. Drawn to marry the Divine Presence, I had ended up estranged" (102).

Intuitions flow like water in this book, laying bare the duplicities of religious thinking. If I were thorough with Taylor's text, I'd need another chapter to explicate them. Most intriguing is that she thinks the Bible holds too much sway in Christian communities. The phenomenon, called bibliolatry, she lays *first* at her own feet. "If I am not careful," she writes, "I can begin to mistake the words on the page for the realities they describe." She continues, "The whole purpose of the Bible is to convince people to set the written word down in order to become living words in the world for God's sake" (107). She's advising people to shelve the book and make their relationships with neighbors, not their reading list, "the substance of faith." Their "willing conversion of ink back to blood"—a lovely phrase—means to imitate biblical models, like Rebekah and Doubting Thomas, whose examples Christians are sketchy at best in following.

THE ISSUE in the 1990s that pushed Taylor to favor community over text split many Episcopals: the ordination of gay and lesbian priests. Taylor, who supported ordination and "learned to feign neutrality" as pastor, discovered that those opposed were basing *their* opinions on the scantest of textual references, a few passages in Leviticus and the Pauline writings, and not, as Taylor hoped, in ethical defense of their actual neighbors. She hoped her congregants would rally round "the very great risk of taking part in stories that are still taking shape" (107). In other words, to recognize that human sexuality is not fixed by creed but keeps evolving.

Further hobbling is members' inability to handle "face-to-face conflict." Taylor notes that "many prefer writing long, single-spaced letters to the rector in lieu of direct confrontation." Moreover, "what they hold most dear" leads the ultra-pious to "avoid confessing their sorest fears by speaking of church doctrine instead or appealing to orthodox Christian belief for support" (109). How many of the brood belonged to Grace-Calvary because of its rigidity, its mulish steadfastness to Bible lore? Too many for Taylor.

The lesson is how fixated many congregants are by the adhesiveness of textual authority and the unawareness with which they determine their associations. These insights *Leaving Church* abounds in. How right Taylor is when she discovers that she was the wrong person for this pastoral appointment. "I realized just how little interest I had in defending Christian beliefs" (109). Too late for that. "My role and my soul were eating each other alive" (111). Time to resign. (One unusual thing about this memoir is that Taylor seems to have endured her tenure, in frustration and self-deception, barely realizing what was happening to her at the time.)

There's much naïveté about spirituality to find in Taylor. What did she expect from semi-orthodox Christians but semi-orthodox Christianity? Isn't that allegiance to doctrine one reason why many agnostic Americans "excuse themselves" from faith-based communities, fearing the uniformity of thought? Isn't that why, in a culture that has politicized institutional membership, most non-Christians today feel that church authorities as well as the conservative rank-and-file are more often than not against LGBTQ identities, women's reproductive rights, and the health of the planet?

By mid-book, she decides to leave.

> If it is true that God exceeds all our efforts to contain God, then is it too big a stretch to declare that *dumbfounded-ness* is what all Christians have most in common? Or that coming together to confess all that we do not know is at least as sacred an activity as declaring what we think we do know? (111)

Imagine a club whose teachings weigh sacred knowledge with an equal call to unbend those teachings when necessary. With such a balance, I understand what it means, in Taylor's phrase, to "become living words" (107). One's expressed values *are* one's living words, which she achieves by reenacting via memoir her earth-supernal link. Thus, spirituality expresses one's lived maneuver through and away from religion to respark one's personal flame. It sounds like a tenet of belief: to raise doubt to the level of faith, a kind of faith *in* doubt. Can one's spirituality be one's own disappointment with the Christian worldview? Can the spiritual be religion's adversary? Is that doublespeak?

For Taylor, the Christ bar is set too high. She writes that pastors have been "presented with Jesus himself as our model, so that most of us could only imagine ourselves disappointing everyone in our lives from God on down" (150). To have practiced and failed at wearing the collar (how apt a word) is a radical end. Aware of her teetering place as an Episcopal, she declares, "By fleeing the church to seek refuge in the world, I had reversed the usual paradigm" (168). Autobiographical Christianity now has an argument at odds with Augustine's certainty and Merton's conversion. Add in Taylor's rejection, and the glass altar cracks.

Grace-Calvary, with help from the author, buried her spirituality. This burial suggests that what we value the most is susceptible far more to our delusions than our judgment. The spade must slice more deeply. Taylor is proof that despite these delusions, the record we offer as probing testament to congenial fantasy has a nascent sacredness of its own.

⚮

BARBARA BROWN Taylor titles her sections "Finding," "Losing," and "Keeping." Of the last, I don't want to give short shrift to the recovery many, Taylor included, find in spiritual discourse. She loses *and* she gains. To the latter: "If my time in the wilderness taught me anything, it is that faith in God has both a center and an edge and that each is necessary for the soul's health." And, "If another loss in the months following my resignation was the loss of Mother Church, I gained a new attachment to the Holy Spirit, which I steadfastly experienced as 'she.'" Taylor lauds (and teaches in her new role as a professor of religious studies) the ceremonies of Native American spirituality, the wisdom litera- ture of other traditions, and her more than tentative clinging to God's abundance and Christ's example. "All these years later," she writes, "there are still a few who believe that becoming fully human is the highest honor they can pay to the incarnate one who showed them how" (230).

One element I do hear in the book's closing is the sacerdotal. I'm not sure what "fully human" means (to have been as wrong as you've been right?) or what Christ's showing "them how" means. Was his crucifixion and resurrection the *how?* The finale finds Taylor reinscribing herself inside the "divine vision" of the Chris- tian God she has helped deinstitutionalize. For her, maybe. But for the flock? Doubtful. Still, Taylor's tale epitomizes the most conspicuous faith-based change in our lifetime: she is spiritual but not religious,[14] even though she continues to lean on the everlasting arms.

On a return visit to Grace-Calvary a few years later, she writes tenderly,

> Walking up the painted gray steps with my uncle, I could feel my heart grow larger in my chest, as if we had suddenly gained more altitude than we had. I tugged on the brass door handle and it opened, allowing us both inside the dollhouse church that I had fallen in love with before I ever met the

people. The day must have been a Saturday, since I could smell the communion bread that someone had left in the sacristy—either that or it was Jesus, coming to me in the form that I had held in my hands so often. That smell alone was enough to tell me that I would never leave church, not really. (225)

The intimate physical detail is a needed turn from her usual explanatory narrative. But is the description just more deception after all the "leaving" she has done prior? Returning, I note the authenticity of touch and smell easily lure her back to the illusion's reality, a real illusion, if you will, that Taylor rather prefers. Or it may be just a wise ambivalence, a neither/nor position through which we disclose the enigmas of our souls to ourselves. One of those enigmas, perhaps the most germane for Taylor, is this: disuniting her Episcopal conviction has led her to spiritual stability.[15]

I KNOW of no contemporary memoir that mixes private shame with divine intervention as ably as Joe Mackall's *The Last Street before Cleveland: An Accidental Pilgrimage* (2006).[16] Indeed, it is the story of how shame opens a path to the divine that the book unspools, like Ariadne's thread. Its deftness and honesty, which I have garnered from multiple readings and lectures on this book, still astound me.

Mackall is nearing forty, in 1997, when Tom, a neighborhood friend from his Cleveland childhood, dies from a "self-administered overdose" of drugs. The death's shock, its "warning about a life wasted," revives Mackall's own lack of purpose, creating the panicky desolation of the book's drama. Adding to his funk is a Catholic boyhood he recalls, replete with altar-boy mishaps, equal parts pathetic and bathetic. In adolescence, he receives an F in religion class; another time, he gets laced on communion wine. In 1979, he abandons the church. It is also the year his mother, a "militant Catholic," dies—but not before he announces to her one day, years earlier at twelve, that he doesn't think he believes anymore. Why not? she asks. "I began telling her," he writes, "about the presence of evil in the world and how could it possibly matter whether I ate meat on Friday and an assortment of other complaints about Catholicism and injustice." Her comeback bristles: "Maybe someday you will" (93). His mother won't argue, and Mackall, decades on, still suffers that slight. One sign of his loneliness as an unbeliever is that he dreams the universe, sapped of all materiality, retains its essence: God. No sooner imagined, however, and he pushes such a fantasy away as delusion.

After Tom's death, Mackall's wayward life smacks him hard. He catalogs his earlier traumas and psychic wounds: the death of his mother, a betrothal he blows off, years wandering away from Cleveland and Ohio and the year he settles back for good, his alcoholism, in which his sobriety is always tested by working-class drinking buddies, and an online-supplied addiction to the painkiller tramadol. Mackall often wonders why his self-control is shot. He is blessed with a great wife, kids, nearby father, faculty position, and more, but he blames himself as "not enough," besieged by an Augustine-like personal loathing.

One thing that sustains Mackall is his passion for reading: "Literature ruled my life. I consulted it for advice. I sought its moral guidance. I worshipped in its riotous quietude" (122). In short, the study of writing is his new religion or, as he puts it, the night his mother died, "I, at least on some subconscious level, shifted my faith from Catholicism to literature" (119). A professor of English, a journalist, and a writer since his twenties, Mackall has time to absorb, even live by, literary wisdom. His most poignant instruction comes from one of J. D. Salinger's *Nine Stories*, "A Perfect Day for Bananafish," which he devours in college. We recall Seymour, the World War II combat veteran who describes to a little girl on a Florida beach a fish that enters an underwater hole and, gorging on bananas, finds itself so fattened it can't escape. The girl looks out at the waves, spies one fish with six bananas in its mouth, and leaves unfazed. Seymour's response? He returns to his hotel room, gets in bed next to his napping wife, and puts a bullet in his brain.

This existential tale swims into Mackall's porous malaise about his "mother's cancer and impending death." Representing his condition, "Bananafish" resounds. The death of those close to us entraps us in their loss and something worse: realizing that we are now more important than anyone else because of our own "impending death."

I wager it's true that art saves us. But it does not follow that we should "believe in" it or use it as "moral guidance." What there is instead, as Mackall demonstrates, is the inner dialogue we are offered by its theme: Seymour's suicide represents *any* suicidal path. Be it through booze, pills, a psychosis, banana engorgement—whatever. The point is, fiction guides us to questions of morality and mortality, but, as Salinger so sadistically implies (here is one man's neat way out), we suffer such quandaries until we can't reconcile them. To cease the mental pain, we choose to die. Or, as Camus argues in *The Myth of Sisyphus*, we also choose not to die. We live on, heroically and absurdly.

Thus, for Mackall, replacing religion with literature teaches him "that stories had the power to change lives, even to save them." In Seymour's case, no. In Mackall's, perhaps.

✣

DESPITE LITERATURE'S balm, Mackall continues to face midlife mania and a tramadol addiction, both dilating his fears more than ever. His crisis moment arrives when he realizes he has "no control over my body. Even less over my mind." It's the end; he's dying, he thinks. And what pops into his head? "The mad urge to pray" (132). Which, of course, part of him denies. Spiritually belittled, he tosses his drugs in a dumpster. A visit to the emergency room and a nervous breakdown of sorts ensue. "And then something happens." Something which he "cannot fully explain" (135).

Before I present *what,* a kind of reverse exorcism, I need to iterate the emotional load with which Mackall writes *Last Street.* First are his complex motivations, determined by past events, and second, the constant prophecy, determined by his personality, that he'll fail. They go hand in hand: I am the person my past has made me; the more I fail, the more I feel destined for future failure. Failure more than success seems, ironically, to map his alienation. As though it's prescribed. Most Americans revolt against such spiritual peonage. There has to be a way out. Confess dependencies, quit drugs, get treatment, write a second act, restart the heart. One punch to the groin (where Salinger and Camus intervene) is realizing that *true* death is death-in-life, Seymour's radical out. Mackall hems and haws. Is his fate the same?

Out walking one morning, in a deep funk, through the halcyon countryside, Mackall's senses open to nature. Note the sudden, unmistakably strong I-statements:

> I listen to the snow squeaking beneath my feet and the geese honking overhead. I hear an Amish horse and buggy in the distance. As the buggy approaches, I'm stunned by the aesthetics of the black horse breathing vapor against the background of a snow-laden field. Having lived for fourteen years in an area of rural Ohio dense with Old Order Amish, I've seen horses and buggies hundreds of times. But something's different. (136)

On its heels come two pages of surprise: "How could I not have noticed the beauty of a red tractor stalled in a dormant cornfield?" It's an awakening that characterizes the verse of the Ohio poet James Wright. (Something about Ohio's ordinariness is extraordinary.) Like a Breughel painting, everything melds into one: the Amish children, an old man driving a pickup, the oak tree's bare branches, the winter vapor, the horse pulling the buggy, the snow, the agelessness. It's all "held together," it's all "one thing," it's all a glimpse "into eternity" (136).

Where has this beauty been hiding? I feel as if I need to bellow this beauty. So I do. I scream. I scream again. No words come out, just an elemental primitive, joyful hollering to the hills.

This is outside the boundaries of my experience. I'm without words to describe it. I have nothing to measure it against.

My personal deus ex machina.

This has to be the love I've never really believed in. The love of the Creator. God's love. (137)

Such is his vision, thirteen pages before the memoir's close. He calls it the "descent of grace," "some version of Paul's great glimpse." The dark events of his life and his "cynical disposition" constitute his "spiritual DNA" (139). As well, this visitation manipulates said DNA into what Mackall calls a love he's "never really believed in." Which suggests it's been there, patiently waiting to manifest itself as *his* belief. It's a conversion, one his personality has finally cleared him *for*. He describes the event as "a moment of piercing the surface of things and [my] being able to see, feel, touch, taste, and hear the giant quiet of divine love" (144).

Piercing the surface of things. This reawakened affinity for the divine some ex-Catholics nurse despite quitting the church as inadequate or false. More keenly, Mackall reminds us that Catholicism demands his assent to dogma, while literature invites his assent to doubt. The Christian myth bequeaths no escape from suffering except through Christ, while literature, a countervailing force, opens the trapdoor out via stories of individual expiation. Literary memoir houses untold themes, but chief among them is conscious atonement. For the writer, I'd stress the *conscious* muscle of atonement. It's not enough to expose one's demons and banish them via confession. It may be enough to inflame that consciousness and get the reader to fully feel those demons. Any more than that is gravy.

Most striking for me is how Mackall has been ensouled by the pantheistic sunrise of God's love. Not God but God's love. Landing on God's love incarnates nothing. Except, perhaps, the words that make God's love so. In this regard, Mackall emphasizes for maybe one-tenth of the book this dramatic and lasting deliverance through which he is valued. The simple beauty of his prose overcomes the malignant spirit he had no idea he himself could overcome.

God's love may redeem Mackall, but it doesn't delink his personality, his past, or his failures from their adamancy. It takes time to awaken, it takes work to stay awake. How do I know God's love on that Amish-bright day with its Polaroid-like amalgam of forces is real? Here's one way: *The Last Street before Cleveland* does not assert that given his travail all will be well. Had that been the outcome, Mackall would have written a devotional, a book of prayer, not a memoir.

IN AN interview,[17] Mackall tells me that the hopelessness he knew prior to his vision went "beyond addiction." It was "spiritual despair." A decade after publication, he remains haunted by two edifices of childhood and adolescence: his working-class origins and his family's Catholicism, those "million rules I couldn't follow." "I wasn't able to see it and I wasn't able to *let* myself feel it." He's since begun to identify his values as working class, "which I never imagined would have any currency with the [university] world I live in now. I allowed it back in. The faith part—I just shut that out completely. And still most days I pretty much live in the nonbelieving state. That's pretty much my default state." The irony he's conscious of is that "there's no real future in" nonbelief. "I know enough about myself that I thought I'd be comfortable with secular humanism. But there's a part of me that needs more."

He cherishes characters like Holden Caulfield, Seymour Glass, and Stingo in William Styron's *Sophie's Choice*. "Those people are as real to me as anybody—just in a different realm. If I thought about it that way I could make the next leap" to faith, "which I thought to survive and to thrive I needed to do." In essence, such canny models got him through the times when the realization of God's love was, for whatever reason, AWOL.

Characters who occupy the imagination are real, Mackall says, because they seem more lifelike than their living counterparts. Certainty in literature's representative actuality means he trusts the art as a reader and teacher and he trusts the writing as an author: "I wasn't going to let religion get in the way of my faith," which, he underlines, is not based in Rome. ("Ninety-nine percent of the time I think religion is the scourge of the planet.")

Nevertheless, he lauds the Christian writer Bret Lott. Lott has written that "Christ's insertion into history combined once and for all story and logic, imagination and reason."[18] For Mackall, the scriptural presence of Jesus in history and in myth means he need not reconcile the literal and the figurative. Christ *is* a literary figure nonpareil; his speech and his actions appear authentic, while his fate is figurative (except to those who believe he was resurrected). Once an author renders a character's actions with veracity, that character's enactment becomes a reality. We never ask if Charles Portis's Rooster Cogburn lived. Why? Because we know he does. In *True Grit*.

What's crucial for Mackall? That love is love, no matter its source, whether abiding in the natural or in the inner world. Wife, granddaughter, Sophie Zawistowska. And the fulcrum to know this is self-love, his core theme. Mackall sees himself as a character in his memoir who transforms, even briefly, his despair. "Its currency" lives on in him. That's a kind of conscious atonement at the heart of the spiritual memoir. Mackall tells me that he re-reads the ending section of *Last Street* when, alienated, dismayed, he needs a kick-in-the-pants rejoinder: Though God's embrace wavers, it is also intrinsic to who he is. Because he felt it that day, and he wrote it back into being.

𝕽

I WANT to take a quick off-ramp and touch on one element that I've tried to ignore but can't—the commercial side of spiritual discourse. Most of us know publishing's factory farm of amateur experts who have found their calling, "authorship"—commodity production, sales objectives, twelve-step programs, and the many guises of the human-potential movement, one of whose billboards is to market the franchise with a "book." It's not only celebrity claptrap and Dr. Oz diets that dominate these advice tomes. It's the *chatter* of people who are aliterate (can read but don't) and who frame themselves as illness-to-lifestyle missionaries. We assume because we've had bariatric surgery or figured out the top five love secrets, we can cobble together a listicle of devotions whose method benefits those as afflicted or lost as we were—which is why we wrote the book and ascended the dais in the first place.

In a culture of platformed spectacles, such drivel is everywhere, life as a Pfizer commercial. I admire the challenge offered by David J. Leigh.[19] What kind of text, anymore, he asks, can "suffice to convey the touch with the sacred"? Of the ten spiritual authors he examines, most of whom relate epiphanies and describe them vividly, Leigh notes that "the concern of these writers will be to find language adequate to their conversion experience in a secularized world where religious language has become the fundamentalist's cliché or the advertiser's stock phrase" (7).

Those B-roll clichés and phrases, as Leigh writes, plant the flag not through poetry or essay; nor are their tonally sacerdotal mini-chapters fledged as memoir. These books avoid tension between self and soul; their chroniclers often mount a pilgrimage to Fatima, Portugal, or a luxury retreat in San Miguel de Allende. On course, they seldom decamp in that long, lonesome valley or down among the darker latitudes. Their authorial tacks resemble each other like swarming bees. The spiritual is fashioned as a program of stress relief, a kind of soul-tasking: spiritual fly-fishing, spiritual cooking, spiritual housecleaning (I did not make any of those up). In the end, *spiritual* means a mindful way of getting things done, like changing your Volvo's sparkplugs.

An example is Sharon Salzberg's *Faith: Trusting Your Own Deepest Experience*,[20] a guidebook to Buddhism. She begins by trying to turn the nigh-indefinable word *faith* on its head: "I want to invite a new use of the word faith, one that is not associated with a dogmatic religious interpretation or divisiveness." She calls her usage "fresh, vibrant, intelligent, and liberating" (xiv). Soon, Salzburg is enumerating the Four Noble Truths, the life of Buddha, stories of his followers, replete with train schedules and boarding times. Disregard, she says, hers or anyone's "dogmatic religious interpretation" of faith, because Buddhism is not a religion. Yet with a "practice" promulgated by adherents like Salzberg, it may as well be: religion lite. Again, it's not that her experience lacks meaning; many have found comfort in her ministry of Eastern traditions. It's that her prose is hackneyed. Utterly disappointing is Salzberg's lack of the puckish metaphor, the original phrase, the rhetorical stamp in which *her* writerly lantern might glow.

In a later chapter, "Despair: The Loss of Faith," twenty years into her practice of loving-kindness meditation, she writes that one day, on retreat, she "entered a realm of suffering that would lead me to reach for a new level of faith." Before any suffering is portrayed, say, a harrowing whodunit or the emotional foundering that might embody something sensuous, she generalizes for three pages on *despair*: "when someone disappoints us grievously"; when "one day we lose our bearings"; when "we feel separate from everyone and everything"; when "we feel devastated and alone"—and then tells us that it's okay that we have had these feelings (100–102). Because she did, too. If there's any momentum in the book, it's decimated by such vacuous explanations. We're not engaging the spiritual; we're being lectured to.

Whatever roadblock Salzberg encounters, the Highway Patrol issues her a waiver to pass on through. When she "argues" that we are miserable because we are closed "to the vastness and mystery of what life provides in each moment" (92), I say, What are you talking about? Who is this "we"? Who do you know is closed to awe or dread? Does anyone really think we appease tragedy by mindfully sitting? It's been too long since that *anyone* read *Siddhartha*. For a philosophy that describes how the root of our suffering is attachment to suffering, this American fix-it machine whose homilies claim to minister to our individual and planetary woe is snake oil.[21]

✌

INTENSITY, SHOCK, disputation are the boastful, telltale attractions of the spiritual writer. It's the drama these attractions unleash, the elusiveness of the ethereal, the drama of the elusive—all of which the best authors craft. This craft comes in Lindbergh's tactuality with the shells at the beach, Matthiessen's obsession as a naturalist compared with his failure as a husband and father, Taylor's throwing her churchliness overboard, Mackall's awe-firm, hard-won love. Note my *descriptors:* the author activates his or her self-agency, one that heads for open water, where the epiphanic likely occurs. What I want is none of the pre-op or post-op salvational moralizing that contending with the ineffable, the anomalous, alas, even the supernatural leads to.

What I want the writer to do is to wrestle. I want a face-off between what is hidden and the ardor with which she gets at that hiddenness without recourse to what anyone else thinks because anyone else does not see things as she does. Generally, the more she sees what others do not see and have not undertaken *as she has*, the better. Above all, I want the writer to wield the memoirist's art (voice, style, diction, emphasis, honesty), turn away from polemical tracts and spirit guides, and turn toward, however perplexing and unruly, the undiscovered self (the phrase is Carl Jung's). This trait is described in Elizabeth Andrew's book *Writing the Sacred Journey:* "As odd as it may seem, moving away from the assumption that you know your material can make the sacred part of it more accessible to your readers."[22]

Andrews's idea rings true: rouse the sacred from its lair by *moving away from the assumption that you know your material.* You've got to be ready to shape-shift—aesthetically and personally—to labor over an authentic but new voice (*yours*) that speaks defiantly and humbly on the page. Spiritual writing—if it is fully enigmatic, reliably unreliable, never reverent—defuses our bafflement only when authors improvise on their stories and reflections in shapes untried.

THE MOST recent and best example of a shape untried I know of is Barbara Ehrenreich's *Living with a Wild God: A Memoir* (2014).[23] Here is one of the most disputatious, spirit-evaluating, probatively researched meditations we have. In May 1959, Ehrenreich, age seventeen, has a mystifying vision, which she grounds in no religious persuasion (she was raised an atheist) and which troubles her no end. One day, while traveling through Lone Pine, California (between Mount Whitney and Death Valley), she dreams of a brain, *her* brain, graphed and analyzed on a large screen by a class of college students. The dream tells her, "This is what you are—a sac of tissue enclosed in membrane, a *thing* like anything else" (109). After two fitful nights, she goes for a walk before dawn and beholds an "image of fire." "The world flamed into life," she writes. "It was a furious encounter with a living substance that was coming at me through all things at once, and one reason for the terrible wordlessness of the experience is that you cannot observe fire really closely without becoming part of it" (116).

Of course, such a hallucination carries a holy portent.

> I knew that the heavens had opened and poured into me, and I into them, but there was no way to describe it, even to myself. As for trying to tell anyone else, should anyone ask where I had disappeared to at dawn—what would I have said? That I had been savaged by a flock of invisible

angels—lifted up in a glorious flutter of iridescent feathers, then mauled, emptied of all intent and purpose, and pretty much left for dead? (117)

At college, studying chemistry and protesting the Vietnam War, Ehrenreich comes back down to earth. She refuses "the vague gurgles of surrender expressed in words like 'ineffable' and 'transcendent.'" She confesses that her "general thought has been: If there are no words for it, then don't say anything about it. Otherwise, you risk slopping into 'spirituality,' which is, in addition to being a crime against reason, of no more interest to other people than your dreams" (115–16).

But even as Ehrenreich warns us off the "slop" of spirituality, her words, "ineffable" and "transcendent," do carry weight as the most common glosses for expressing the inscrutable realm. Ehrenreich's head trip *was* transcendent: she merged with the living substance of fire. That's her description at first glance, necessarily imprecise. She even says that "the truth" of the fire's heat that day would have "two conditions attached to it: one, that you can never speak of it, even to yourself, and two, that you can never fully recapture it ever again" (119). Such is *not* the calling of the memoirist. Indeed, those "you can never" injunctions compel life-writers to pursue the uncapturable, the Other, as if on a dare.

MUCH OF *Wild God* is spent hunting what this Other—the imagined or actual force that brought the vision—might be. Possible explanations are (not in order) an epileptic seizure, an epiphany, a moment of madness, mental illness, depression, alienation, atheism, psychosis, even schizophrenia.

With epilepsy, she finds that the apparition may have occurred when "large numbers of neurons start firing in synchrony, until key parts of the brain are swept up in a single pattern of activity, an unstoppable cascade of electrical events, beginning at the cellular level and growing to encompass the entire terrain that we experience as 'consciousness'" (123). This throe suggests a momentary seizure, but it doesn't map any chronic condition she has since suffered. She also speculates on the encounter as a schizophrenic episode, but discovers, again, she has none of its recurring symptoms.

As her writing career grows—and left-wing causes, marriage, children, divorce, and their attendant worries intrude—she is diagnosed with and treated for depression. Though the skirmish in Lone Pine remains vexing, she avows that a flash of the inexplicable could not have prefigured her depression. That illness comes from one's family and one's predisposition for the disease. Depression is not triggered by lights at dawn. Playing the God card, partly for fun, she imagines the salvational chumminess of a Pentecostal church where co-seers "did not find you crazy" (137). Glory, hallelujah might settle it. Then again, it might not.

She argues that her commitment to atheism may have augured the fiery element. In other words, she awoke to what her conscious disbelieving mind would not allow, a sort of nonverbal signal that God was speaking to her via a mirage. But, recalling atheist friends who've reported on their own otherworldly episodes, Ehrenreich acknowledges that such revelations do not turn unbelievers into believers. Unbelievers demand evidence, especially when the unknowable seems impenetrable. More important—and Ehrenreich is a clear example—the mystical presses for greater inquiry, not less. Atheism, she sees, didn't gin up the phantasm in the sky, either.

Further on her journey, Ehrenreich wonders if her vision shares anything with the five notorious prophets who were stricken by God's lightning—Abraham, Moses, Jesus, Paul, and Mohammed. Current psychological theory notes that while these men may have suffered "diseases," schizophrenia perhaps, their shamanic cargo pinpoints a core adaptation in our evolution. Ehrenreich calls it "an innate propensity to error" (222). Another definition might be self-deception as a means of surviving. I would add to this definition, our willingness to elevate, even worship, such deception. How?

Those who ply error, whether conscious or not, rationalize superstitions as socially beneficial. That one most mystic person in the tribe—who warned that a grass-moving wave across the surrounding savannah was a pride of male lions approaching, their nostrils alive with the stench of human flesh, hoping to chow down on a disease-ridden people—became the seer. These seers or holy men called themselves all-knowing and soon used their gift to assign divine intent to the lions. Thus, the moving grasslands, which might have been the big cats themselves or the peerless majesty of the wind, were deemed beasts of retribution, sent by Moloch to eat the children, no doubt based on some inscrutable slight of the tribe's doing.

Under the seer or shaman's guidance, we man the perimeter because the Deity—the inexplicable—has his devouring eye upon us. Metaphysical thinking (call it poetry) becomes viable, and, as a testament to the mind's malleability, the metaphysical soon balances if not overrules the quotidian. This "propensity for error" we carry—to think that what is not there must be there—becomes, in the end, Ehrenreich's explanation for the "fire of heaven."

She also terms the propensity for error *predation*. Whatever it was she saw aflame in Lone Pine demonstrates the common, ancient fear in humans that we are being hunted not just by animals larger than us, which indeed was the case, but also by imagined and willful agents many times deadlier than a tiger's mauling. These agents include the tendency to see the face of God in a cumulus cloud formation or to hear a roll of thunder from the mountains as a response to one's malicious thought. Neuroscientists call this fear-bent brain component the hyperactive agency detection device (HADD), and it's centered in the amygdala (222).[24] This module provides one way of explaining religious ordeals as an adaptive trait in human evolution. (Of course, what makes this trait difficult to recognize, let alone accept, is that we no longer live on a savannah full of lions in competition for food. We live in a culture whose reality *is* media, that is, a reality mediated by the prison of technology and the devices we are addicted to.)

Our anxiety with ISIS, and with terrorism in general, proves that hyperactive detection is still shudderingly present. Interest groups like political parties and white nationalists stoke loyalty because of the fear of invasion and annihilation by foreigners just as the ancients did. The Threat of the Other makes the movie-going masses think Wonder Woman will punch out any Earth-bound meteors. Waking up, we deconstruct just how hyperactive our illusionary consciousness is. Which is where Ehrenreich ends her memoir.

She asserts that ambiguity—and its behavioral grounding—is a major turn in hominid speciation and useful in decoding experience. We know two things are true: (1) those "agents out there" rule us because we attribute to them not only a body but also a benign or an evil intent; (2) our modules of self- and social deceit are adaptive features that insist we retain both—our fantasies are as real as our realities are fantastic.

This balanced equation suggests that evolution has wired our encounters with protective misjudgment. Apropos of "error," we are learning that our approach to mystery has exhausted the Age of Enlightenment and is now tobogganing toward a new science of plasticity or brain-wiring. God, according to one contemporary and less soulful view, is an adaptation expressed not to a being but to neurological circuitry that makes God exist as much as makes God not exist.

Ambiguity and the inexplicable—confirmed via Ehrenreich's cognitive-based research—are human traits, not lightning bolts of divine intervention. Ambiguity helps regulate our bullshit meter, which too often, via fear of annihilation or hope of salvation, goes haywire and turns bullshit into the Rapture. The lesson is, we need not encumber the inscrutable—Gaia, deep time, dark matter, dark energy, God of the gaps—with abstract thought or abject dread. We can denature otherness, welcome its known and unknown unknowns. Centuries of such welcoming (to come) lessen the predatory nature of the Other, in effect, deracinate our hyperactive detection devices and may one day get rid of them entirely. This other innate propensity, our long-grown and long-horned negative capability, which Ehrenreich has deduced, is the best of all possible explanations for her vision.

🦋

THROUGHOUT THIS fourth chapter, I've tried to show that spiritual writers often grieve an emotional wound, begun in a religious or mystical context, that typically a long prose work assuages. Ehrenreich's book assuages the disruption she has lived with since her vision at age seventeen. Rendering the nagging anxiety of this event in memoir doesn't make her more spiritual. Rather, Ehrenreich's attempt to unmask the fiery vision makes her more *herself*, which is the goal of this writing: to let art ensoul us and let the power of personal narrative help us individuate as people and as artists.

I want to close with a few thoughts about our current sensibility toward spiritual literature.

A good beginning (and end) is Roland Barthes's 1968 Red Sea parting of the readerly text and the writerly text. The distinction he first parsed in *S/Z: An Essay* and elaborated in his essay "The Death of the Author."[25] The readerly text Barthes calls a finished creation, a "product," whose exemplum is the article, the essay, the book. He says that such work has been written by "the Author," a creator who, "when believed in, is always conceived of as the past of his own book: book and author stand automatically on a single line divided into a *before* and an *after*. The Author is thought to *nourish* the book, which is to say that he exists before it, thinks, suffers, lives for it, is in the same relation of antecedence to his work as a father to his child" (145).

The writerly text is built on "ourselves writing," which, Barthes says, is the act of pushing the pen or clacking the keys, a live act, a thinking-through, an improvisation, the unfinished thing its finish: "The modern scriptor is born simultaneously with the text, is in no way equipped with a being preceding or exceeding the writing, is not the subject with the book as predicate; there is no other time than that of the enunciation and every text is eternally written *here and now*" (145).

Mirabile dictu: Barthes's writerly text intersects, hand in glove, with my ideas about spiritual writing. In its ever-materializing improvisation, writing "has no other content . . . than the act by which it is uttered" (146). Writing is a doing just as life is a doing. Once it's done, it reveals. What it reveals is, in a sense, itself, but also the tensions and displacements it takes to manifest revelations of consequence. As Barthes writes, this consequence, in turn, "liberates what may be called an anti-theological activity, an activity that is truly revolutionary since to refuse to fix meaning is, in the end, to refuse God and his hypostases—reason, science, law" (147).

It is arguable whether God is the bearer of *fixed meaning*, a hypostasis or irreducible essence all his own. But I get Barthes's intention loud and clear: writing is designed not merely to refuse God but to disentangle the meaning of God, reason, science, and law, things we do well to question, dispute, *unfix*. Which, in terms of reason, science, law, and even spirituality, I think we do.

After Barthes, I surmise that spiritual writing—largely because of the newness I've been trying to articulate—possesses no a priori form, a surprise that I hope stays surprising. The tracks of past literary form (readerly) and present authorial invention (writerly) cross on rare occasion. David Shields and Jonathan Lethem have recently made new texts, or assemblages, by copying or plagiarizing old texts. But readerly/writerly cannot replicate each other. Perhaps I've labored under a misconception, assuming the "spiritual memoir" shares some/many of its traits with its sire, religious autobiography. Such is the seduction of applying any teleological deduction to literary evolution.

This postredemptive development in the confessional canon is new. The spiritual memoir has evolved and is now pushing its "form," if you will, toward wilder improvisations and riskier fact/fiction mergers. Rhetorical freewheeling suggests that personal narrative need not be religious or spiritual or heroic (Peter Matthiessen,

Barbara Ehrenreich), even as some fellow travelers (Mirabai Starr, Pema Chödrön) are given to catechism, meditation, pilgrimage. I realize we are only now inaugurating the spiritual memoir as a subgenre in Western literature. But *any* memoir worth its extemporized soul volcanizes the inner life, by turns impolitic and inscrutable and random.

A final reason to leave the spring windows of spiritual writing open is to encourage tempest-tossed anomalies of the essay, the linked-essay collection, and the memoir. I seldom weary of these works—although I do quit those that goose the page with remedies or sermons. I don't care to reprimand the failures. I'd rather laud the successes, not just the work—whose value is intrinsic—but also the libidinal pleasures of engaging the unanswerable stuff. How do we live creatively under threat of these grand, troublesome vexations: the barely apprehensible realities of geologic time, molecular complexity, the spacetime continuum, the afterlife and the before-life or neither as the case may be, accepting our dying graciously, the rare numinous ping when we feel anything (peace, grace, healing) is possible, the slow strangulation of the planet, or the concrete and abstract nature of language itself?

NOTES

1. John D. Barbour, "Autobiography," in *Encyclopedia of Religion*, 2nd ed., vol. 2 (Farmington Hills, MI: Thomson Gale, 2005).

2. Gems include Terry Tempest Williams, *Refuge: An Unnatural History of Family and Place* (New York: Pantheon Books, 1991); Nancy Mairs, *Ordinary Time: Cycles in Marriage, Faith, and Renewal* (Boston: Beacon Press, 1993); Sidney Poitier, *The Measure of a Man: A Spiritual Autobiography* (San Francisco: HarperSanFrancisco, 2000); Gregory Orr, *The Blessing* (San Francisco: Council Oak Books, 2002); Fenton Johnson, *Keeping Faith: A Skeptic's Journey* (Boston: Houghton Mifflin, 2003); Mary Rose O'Reilley, *The Love of Impermanent Things: A Threshold Ecology* (Minneapolis: Milkweed Editions, 2006); Elizabeth Gilbert, *Eat, Pray, Love: One Woman's Search for Everything across Italy, India, and Indonesia* (New York: Penguin Books, 2006); Hope Edelman, *The Possibility of Everything* (New York: Ballantine Books, 2009); Hamilton Cain, *This*

Boy's Faith: Notes from a Southern Baptist Upbringing (New York: Crown, 2011); Richard Rodriguez, *Darling: A Spiritual Autobiography* (New York: Penguin Books, 2013); Mirabai Starr, *Caravan of No Despair: A Memoir of Loss and Transformation* (Boulder, CO: Sounds True, 2015); Jessie van Eerden, *The Long Weeping: Portrait Essays* (Asheville, NC: Orison Books, 2017), among other jewels.

3. Anne Morrow Lindbergh, *Gift from the Sea* (New York: Pantheon, 1955).

4. Geoffrey Galt Harpham, "Conversion and the Language of Autobiography," in *Studies in Autobiography*, ed. James Olney (New York: Oxford University Press, 1988).

5. Dani Shapiro, *Devotion: A Memoir* (New York: Harper Perennial, 2010).

6. Annie Dillard, *Pilgrim at Tinker Creek* (New York: Harper and Row, Perennial Library Edition, 1985).

7. Other spiritual mavericks share this calling to intention, a pilgrimage to self in nature's unforgiving context. Edward Abbey in *Desert Solitaire: A Season in the Wilderness* (New York: Simon and Schuster, 1968) essays on the political tension between our love of deserts and the fragile desert ecology itself, to know how to preserve that which we should not occupy. *Zen and the Art of Motorcycle Maintenance* by Robert Pirsig (New York: William Morrow, 1974) relives the author's two-wheel spiritual journey into the American Northwest and the ineffable concept of "quality," what makes good writing and what the Good is in the context of motorized transcendence. *Crazy Brave* by Joy Harjo (New York: W. W. Norton, 2012) focuses on the spiritual legacy that comes via her ancestors' voices and their palliative presence during her many crises.

Other socially confrontational memoirs, which may also be described as eco-spiritual, include those by Terry Tempest Williams, Wendell Berry, Gary Snyder, Ann Zwinger, Sigurd Olson, Aldo Leopold, Gretel Ehrlich, and Helen Macdonald.

8. Cheryl Strayed, *Wild: From Lost to Found on the Pacific Crest Trail* (New York: Vintage Books, 2013).

9. Peter Matthiessen, *The Snow Leopard* (New York: Penguin Classics, 1987).

10. *The Snow Leopard* was originally published in two parts in the *New Yorker* (March 27 and April 3, 1978). The following year, the expanded book won the National Book Award for Nonfiction.

11. Ernest Wood, "Seeing into One's Self-Nature," *Zen Dictionary* (Boston: Charles E. Tuttle, 1957), 118.

12. There is no shortage of pithy quotations from Wittgenstein. For instance, "The real question of life after death isn't whether or not it exists, but even if it does what problem this really solves."

13. Barbara Brown Taylor, *Leaving Church: A Memoir of Faith* (Harper San Francisco, 2007).

14. I brought this up briefly in the opening section. I want to take another stab at the meaning of the phrase "but not." First, if we think about the time of prereligious or pagan people, before a "religion" divided its course in miracles from life itself, the same material artifacts, the same fears and myths and joys and sorrows about human, animal, and planetary travail existed and, of their own volition, evoked (rather easily I would think) the spiritual realm, mysterious as well as stingy. I doubt the spiritual realm, in its rare coming and going, had to pick and choose the most or least religious among us on whom to wreak its havoc, to descale our eyes, to remind us of its nonhuman dominion. And second, how odd that no one claims the reverse of this phrase—I'm religious but not spiritual.

15. In 2009, Taylor published *An Altar in the World: A Geography of Faith* (San Francisco: HarperOne). Largely advice-giving, the book feels as though it was contemplated in the margins while she was editing *Leaving Church*, a few years earlier. Each of *Altar*'s twelve chapters begins with "The Practice of," as in "The Practice of Saying No." Her style remains grounded and winning, but it also sounds like a quick turnaround: she seems to want to make a "system" of her fall from religion and her rebirth in spirituality. She is honest. She misses her pastoral role. And she remains permeated with religious conviction. The idea is to apply the private virtues she gained as a self-outcast from Episcopalianism and revivify those virtues in a new community without the Christian clubbishness that drove Taylor to bolt. But be warned: there is, in *Altar*, no larger narrative and very little of the dynamic inner exploration of the previous book.

16. Joe Mackall, *The Last Street before Cleveland: An Accidental Pilgrimage* (Lincoln: University of Nebraska Press, 2006).

17. August 29, 2016.

18. Bret Lott, *Letters and Life: On Being a Writer, On Being a Christian* (Wheaton, IL: Crossway, 2013), 27.

19. David J. Leigh, *Circuitous Journeys: Modern Spiritual Autobiographies* (New York: Fordham University Press, 2000).

20. Sharon Salzberg, *Faith: Trusting Your Own Deepest Experience* (New York: Riverhead Books, 2002).

21. For the great paradoxes of Buddhism and suffering, see Alan Watts, especially *The Way of Zen* (New York: Pantheon Books, 1957).

22. Elizabeth J. Andrew, *Writing the Sacred Journey: The Art and Practice of Spiritual Memoir* (Boston: Skinner House Books, 2005), 19.

23. Barbara Ehrenreich, *Living with a Wild God: A Memoir* (New York: Twelve, 2014).

24. See Evan D. Murray, Miles G. Cunningham, and Bruce H. Price, "The Role of Psychotic Disorders in Religious History Considered," *Journal of Neuropsychiatry and Clinical Neurosciences* 24, no. 4 (2012).

25. Roland Barthes, "The Death of the Author," in *Image Music Text* (New York: Hill and Wang, 1977).

Writing Spiritually

A Rough Guide

> The idea might have been put there by God, I
> thought. Or perhaps the idea *was* God. But not the
> traditional God. A god of self-will. A god of language
> and ideas. An internal voice god. Me, in other words.
>
> —*Veronica Chater,*
>   Waiting for the Apocalypse

At the close of *Wild*'s fourth section—there are five in all—Cheryl Strayed merges the person she was with the person she has become on the Pacific Crest Trail. Almost on cue, the moment arrives when she spots a deer grazing on azaleas. As they share creaturely eye contact, Strayed tells the animal, "You're safe in this world." Then, just as quickly, deer and woman part company. The sudden encounter, coming at the midpoint of her hike, springs an equally sudden memory of her father whom she'd known little about: "He was there, but invisible, a shadow beast in the woods; a fire so far away it's nothing but smoke." Still, his absence has troubled and amazed her all her life. "Of all the wild things, his failure to love me the way he should have had always been the wildest thing of all" (233).

She realizes immediately that meeting the deer mirrors her condition. She's the trespasser. She's the one who's learned how to survive in the woods. She can, at last, intrude on what's wild and unresolved in *her* life. Survival and recalling her father's thoughtlessness forge a bond. As she disturbs and passes by the deer, time collapses, and the spirit that unites past and present awakens. The moment pacifies her inner (and book-long) turbulence. She cries, her first tears on the trail, in two-and-a-half months. Suddenly, the yoke of her burdened memory loosens: "I didn't have to be amazed by him anymore. There were so many other amazing things in this world." She weeps neither from happiness nor sadness. She cries "because I was full." The tears, in turn, find a corollary in this reckoning sentence: "I felt fierce and humble and gathered up inside, like I was safe in this world too" (234).

Gathered up.

Here, the passive verb—we wonder who or what is doing the gathering—signals an inner, perhaps unconscious process already underway. At last, Strayed is remade by the raw emotions—ecstasy, regret, confusion, anger, uncertainty—which have boiled to the surface after two months of trekking. (What's been mounting up in her body over her twenty-six years is further intensified by what's been pounding her legs and feet every day.) Past/present feelings are piled, stored, ripened, and ready to coalesce, and they burst like an overfilled dam from the pressure. For anything to be gathered up, Strayed first must have felt some force stitching them together. And she does, she tells us: so much so that she is "full."

Such moments in a memoir are rare and decisive. They reveal a psychic purpose that has grown in us, in the seeker, while traipsing endless switchbacks at eight thousand feet. We carry many unreconciled emotions about our pasts, which we think we have misplaced but are, in fact, gut-level present in us all along—until something, stress, typically, activates them. That something produces a catharsis which gathers those emotions into a "fullness," from which we either flee or we are changed. Changed from within and from without.

How do we know the writer has felt these unreconciled emotions? Read the prose aloud. You hear the author feeling the words or you don't. Rely on the descriptive and narrative thrust of the book. If it sounds like a flyover, you'll know. If it sounds as though the pilot has landed the plane, gotten out, and begun hacking her way through the jungle, you'll know. I can't quote the entire scene, but read the chapter, near the end of *Wild*, "Into a Primal Gear." It's a harrowing few hours when two inept, lost men molest Strayed for water and she helps them, even though one hassles her with sexual innuendo. The affront pushes her too close to what may be the most unexpected peril in the wilderness—male assault.

This series of Strayed's fully dramatized encounters, ratcheting up her deliverance back into the world, are crafted to merge the hike's dangerous moments with the writing's aesthetic moments. This is core to any nonfictionist who hopes to write spiritually.

What do I mean?

Writing spiritually often begins as imitation, especially when your subject is so personal, so unverifiable, so open to criticism, and so potentially airy-fairy that to keep it within the orbit of the possible, you need to follow a religious prototype, like Thomas Merton or Anne Lamott. So tortuous is the climb, so bleak are your resources, you may have to. But you may also trust that the tools of literary craft will guide you as well. Given that you've learned them.

Anything you achieve in the "regular" memoir, you achieve in the spiritual memoir. In the latter, however, you are more dependent on technique than the "standard" memoirist is. Why? Because the abstract realm, the private vision, and the means of holding onto something fleeting and uncaptured require you to embody its inexplicableness in a convincing story and in telling detail so you'll know—so your readers will know—what the inexplicable is, exactly.

I have this sense sometimes that there is a being in my home, zipping down our hallway at lightning speed. The being doesn't

seem to care if I ponder its presence. But the fact that I *do* ponder
that presence is what vexes me. First, I wonder whether stating
that a specter is zipping through my home, always down the hallway and past my office door, makes any sense. I doubt it. It's too
private, too immaterial, too much the standard apparition. But it's
true; I feel haunted. I can't shake the feeling. I'm being visited. And
then, letting my imagination loose, it hits me: the thing zipping
through, as though it's on fire, is the spirit of my mother, Dorothy
Wallin Larson. Dead since 1994, my mother was the most painfully
reserved, depressed, fearful, and untouchable person I have ever
known. That she and my father raised my brothers and me passably
well only complicates the matter. She has become the spirit of the
person, in my life most easily associated with women, who lacks
agency. She is the spirit of the person who unhappily accepts her
lot and suffers. She is the spirit of the person who got up every day
and saw to someone else's needs. The spirit of resentment. Because
I have written at length about other people, within and outside of
my family, I have known well—and written very little about her—
my mother is trapped in my psyche, or, better, she visits me now
and again with the breezy reminder that she *is* trapped. And only I,
the writer, can free her.

It's almost maudlin, I'm aware. But my mother represents the
deadliness of the vacuous, unwanted, uncalled life. She is, in all
her aching reticence, the spirit of that vacuity. That I feel called
to a profession and to an art—and she did not—troubles me no
end. Troubles and amazes me, like Strayed and her father, enough
to have more than a (psychic) hand in creating that figure dash-
ing down the hallway. Making this little overture to her shows
how I (and how you might, as well) see where writing spiritually
begins.

I KNOW from teaching, from study, and from writing (decades
now) that the elements which the best spiritual writers employ will

guide your efforts. Here, then, is a primer that I hope helps launch and nourish your endeavor.

The spiritual memoir, like any memoir, is backboned on the qualitative practices of narrative, reflective, and expository nonfiction.

They are

(1) a dramatic, substantive, and forthright story;

(2) a series of episodic, consequential scenes;

(3) an experientially dynamic and maturing first-person narrator;

(4) a skillful use of telling details, which, in turn, prompts comparative tropes;

(5) a complement of lyrical and expository styles;

(6) a persuasive load, a confessional tone, a road free from righteousness;

(7) a narrator/writer covenant, signed to elicit the reader's trust;

(8) a sense that whatever you are after likely ends up unrelated to what the writing has to say about whatever it is you are after.

These elements are painstakingly learned and punishingly applied, trial and error, via the backaching joy of revision, until awakened in us is the memoir's latent goodwill. These elements jumpstart the writer's literary craft, imaginative experimentation, moral sensibility, and a willful stick-to-itiveness that insists his or her honesty is the measure of all things.

To reach the goal, we don't need the writer outlining his cross-to-bear or bragging of his nearness to Jesus. We don't need the mansplaining. We need the grit. We need the blisters. We need the oatmeal boiling over the pot's top and dripping down its sides, the high-country hiker's hunger temporarily allayed. We need the quotidian boredom, the incisive terror. We need drama, a ten-episode series from Netflix. Above all, we need doubt dramatized in episodes that ring true to life and ring true to the author's reflections, whether arising from exceptional or commonplace events. In addition to doubt, we need faith—in things felt, in things earned. We need, if possible, the unnamable in-between. Nailing down an expressive language—direct, detailed, forthright—is where spirituality lies: in the unscrolling of the words themselves.

(1) *Typically, a spiritual memoir dramatizes a substantive story with rising and falling action based in a recognizably architectural scheme, developing a particular phase of the life, not its entirety. Still, no mannequin form models all such books. The spirit especially loves working outside the lines.*

If the story is big, then that bigness requires you fit into the prose flashes of, and sudden entries into, the beyond, albeit judiciously. To write a memoir about one year in your life, say, the year you rowed the coast of Maine alone in a canoe, you cannot have breakthroughs occur every afternoon at three sharp. Sure, you have your insights sneak into the quotidian. But, over the course of a year, there can barely be more than one or two or three soul leaps. Moreover, the rarity of those leaps is inversely proportional to their significance.

Mary Karr's *Lit* (2009) is a big story in need of a big book.[1] In her twenties, Karr, when not drunk, is miserable. Her pen has stalled and her marriage is bottoming out. She is taken in by Alcoholics Anonymous, where she learns she can beat the disease with prayer. And beat it she does—after years of bingeing and self-loathing (though her writerly ingenuity never leaves her), she's often on her "effing knees," begging the deity for sobriety. The slog from one state to the other is convincing, in part, because her brass-button style makes her a narrative-*dominant* writer. Everything "happens" as scene in the book; little is reflected on or understood—in the moment or beyond. "Rather than thinking about spiritual practices, arguing them out in my head," she writes, "I almost automatically try them" (297). She's instinctually prayerful. "*Thanks, whoever the fuck you are, I say, for keeping me sober*" (275). "Little Mary Karr, sinner deluxe" (349). Among other motivational digs.

At first, her suddenly alit "spiritual condition," which, watered by meetings and women's groups and phone check-ins and morning supplications, decouples her from the bottle. This turn then turns Catholic with mass, catechism, baptism, and conversion. In the fold, Karr calms family vendettas, becomes a better mother, is saner, happier, though none of it can save her marriage. "The spiritual lens," she notes, "is starting to rewrite the story of my life in the present, and I begin to feel like somebody snatched out of the fire, salvaged, saved" (304).

Karr is among the hardest-working writers in the memoir biz. Her ultralapidary style, her reformed-drunk religiosity, and her confessional sedulousness (nearly four hundred pages) make us hyperaware that whatever she does (writing, dating, parenting, drinking, not drinking), she thinks she never does it well enough. She drives a bandwagon of self-mythology that kudzus the page until we are exhausted, convinced. Then, in case we didn't get it, she adds more. All of it has to be "lived." Physically, seldom psychically. And, at the highest-pitched moments, her entanglements lead somewhere miraculous: "It's a stone fact," she writes, "that—within a week or so of my starting to pray—a man I don't know calls me from the Whiting Foundation to give me a thirty-five-thousand-dollar prize I hadn't applied for" (225).

In the end, Karr's memoir is 98 percent story, 2 percent platitude. (No wonder readers love it!) What spiritual growth resembles for Karr is the long march it took to find that which she is genuinely surprised to be writing about. What it lacks you can guess: the writer questioning the character of the narrator. Reflection is stunted; perhaps it's unnecessary, redundant. Mostly, after recounting her prayerful intervention, she dervishly whirls to the next moment of calamity and redemption. Which is to say, the most important thing is not her debating truth but that her inebriation is Christianly ministered to.

Lit is a marvelous monument to an ego, willful and surrendered. But it's not the only choice the writer has. As I say, you may try a nonnarrative structure. Books by such mavericks as Christian

Wiman, Chet Raymo, Jessie van Eerden, and others are experimental, innovative, iconoclastic. Eschewing the big-sky adventure, they sharpen mythic or theological or scientific perspectives about spiritual possibility as much in belief as in fact as in fictional license. In Raymo's *When God Is Gone, Everything Is Holy: The Making of a Religious Naturalist,*[2] the author launches a meandering and segmented essay with a credo, one that signposts the tale-less structure he's devised:

> I am an atheist, if by God one means a transcendent Person who acts willfully within the creation. I am an agnostic in that I believe our knowledge of "what is" is partial and tentative—a tiny flickering flame in the overwhelming shadows of our ignorance. I am a pantheist in that I believe empirical knowledge of the sensate world is the surest revelation of whatever is worth being called divine. I am a Catholic by accident of birth. (22)

(2) Writers build a story with propulsion and inevitability via scenic episodes, which, as they accumulate, reveal subtle and strong shifts in the narrator's growing spiritual sensibility.

Beverly Donofrio, in *Looking for Mary: Or, The Blessed Mother and Me,*[3] hopes to revivify her lost Catholic faith after thirty-five years of apostasy, cheapened by a penchant to run with male losers, Pamplona-style. She despairs because she feels unworthy and stupid for having thrown away the Catholic's ace in the hole—grace.

As a wild teenager, she quits the church; she has an abortion; at seventeen she marries a dope who soon leaves her with their child; she has a further string of dimwitted lovers. All this until a generation later her seventeen-year-old son, Jason, pinned by his mother's bad decisions, confronts her: "I never ask for things because I'm afraid you'll say no. . . . You're a selfish person" (173). Such, she realizes, she's had coming. She tells herself she'll make amends with a pilgrimage to the shrine in Medjugorje, Croatia, where the Virgin Mary's apparition regularly appears.

What makes this memoir so compelling are the beefy chapters that mix present and past, which center on Donofrio's contrition and her wish to be absolved of so many mistakes. In chapter 10, a twenty-page multistop journey, Donofrio, arriving in Medjugorje, tells a priest at confession about her decades of sin. She recalls—and depicts in a series of scenes—Jason's single meeting with his AIDS-dying father, Ray, and how she reluctantly accompanies Jason to Ray's funeral, after which he calls his mother selfish. She takes Jason to meet Ray's loving ex-wife and her two daughters, also children of the dead father whose bad choices rained down on them as well. After Donofrio enrolls in a Los Angeles New Age church, she listens to a merciful sermon, prays, sings, unpacks her rosary, and realizes it's been twenty-eight years to the day since she married Ray: "I also remembered that I had been depressed on every April 27 for twenty-eight years" (179). Finally, ending the chapter, she is exhausted but hopeful, back where she began, in Medjugorje, postconfession, crying in bed.

The whole traffic jam of memories and depictions has been essential—a tour de force—in playing out Donofrio's reasons for traveling to Croatia, for reviving her religious identity, for the scald of grief, not only on behalf of Jason, whose life she has tainted, but, surprisingly, on behalf of Ray, who "was a sweet and dear person," who was "damaged," and who "suffered more than anyone he ever hurt." She is only now ready to forgive him after nearly three unconscious decades. The next day, she takes communion, this time honestly declaring, "Lord, I am not worthy to receive you, but only say the word and I shall be healed" (180). As I say, grace.

Imagine these words in the analytic voice of a theologian who treats them as one of any ritual utterances *good* Catholics *should* say "with conviction." Not a chance. Here we have an accumulation, which I've spelled out, pressing toward an inexorable climax: Donofrio becomes the object of a destinal Catholicism, still embedded in her, and, perhaps, the only thing that can redeem her.

So many spiritual writers are turned less by the surprise of new vistas or gurus, diets or alien occupations, and more by reimagining their fate. If this be your story, tell it in scenes, which intermingle past and present in their providential codependency.

To iterate: Arriving far from where you begin the trek is key. Dwell in the additive ongoingness that more story leads one to more essence. Take the time to back the boulder down the hill one terrace at a time. Generate a multiplicity of sentences and paragraphs, sections and scenes, arguments and themes, before you try and realize where in the basin of your consciousness you are going.[4]

(3) *The author's character cannot be the narrator's character. The latter is a newly made "I" who has her own up-down-sideways life waiting to be discovered and disclosed—in the gutsiness of the narrator's story and the unveiling of the author's reflection.*

One thing many memoirists don't get is that you have to *portray* the spirit-seeking side of yourself, its sensibility and its veils. The person you create is the you who's been stripped of her public persona. You present this private person and *emphasize* the traits that stipulate her honesty (perhaps a whale or a tadpole of difference from your "real life"), and, to do this, like the stage actor, you must *project*.

Take the travail of Mother Teresa. The woman spent her adulthood serving others in her order, the Missionaries of Charity. A church loyalist, she was *against* abortion and contraception and *for* an "aesthetic" approach to poverty, famously intoning in 1981: "I think it is very beautiful for the poor to accept their lot, to share it with the passion of Christ. I think the world is being much helped by the suffering of the poor people."[5] Because of her political savvy, her persona forced her to deny publicly what her heart told her was true. How shocked many of us were to learn of her inner misery, whose testimony emerged in letters published after she died of heart ailments in 1997. Her secret was that having spent fifty years asking for guidance from God and Christ, neither ever acknowledged her prayers. Their answer was their absence. Nearly all her life, she felt, according to one friend, "no presence of God whatsoever."

She asks in an undated letter to Jesus (the creative punctuation is hers):[6]

> Where is my faith?—even deep down, right in there is nothing but emptiness & darkness.—My God—how painful is this unknown pain. It pains without ceasing.—I have no faith.—I dare not utter the words & thoughts that crowd in my heart—& make me suffer untold agony. So many unanswered questions live within—I am afraid to uncover them—because of the blasphemy—If there be God,—please forgive me.—Trust that all will end in Heaven with Jesus.— When I try to raise my thoughts to Heaven—there is such convicting emptiness that those very thoughts return like sharp knives & hurt my very soul.—Love—the word—it brings nothing. (187)

Ouch. To have carried her despair along with the laundry bags and the bowls of lentil soup is nigh unthinkable—yet how effortlessly the despair flows in the letter's nihilistic phrases. You can hear in her style her estrangement: The more she writes, the sharper the loss. *As though she's writing the loss into being.* Through such writing, her private and embarrassed self is freed; the diary gnome gives her a voice that, except for the psychopathic author, refuses to lie. (Lies trouble us enough in our lives; in memoir, we let them go, the hypocrisy we've lived by and denied, outed.) The virtue of Mother Teresa's character blossoms in letters where she tenders that virtue. As her thoughts unfold, she disarms her pretentions. Perhaps the facility to write leads to greater candidness when prayer does not.

One more thing: Mother Teresa's missionary training taught her to embrace the poor, which she did compassionately. However, her inner life, attested to in letters barred from public exposure while she lived, epitomizes the tension inherent in her order's rules. Contrast her writing with that of Thérèse of Lisieux and you see that while they share the same religion, they do not share the same spirituality.

(4) *Details that ground and metaphors that loft are essential in describing what we hope to communicate about spirit-summoning things, in themselves often indescribable.*

The old saw is, details must tell, which is to say, you paint purple-and-orange flames onto the front sides and hood of your 1956 Chevrolet to announce your arrival (back then) as a young buck burning to be seen. These details do two things: they actualize what's concrete, and they accentuate what's representable.

With spiritual writing, you want the detail to *tell* something about yourself that you the narrator don't yet comprehend and that is not easily apparent in the sensate world. Which objects and environments in your surroundings have drawn you to dialogue between the inner self and concrete objects? As you begin to attach concrete nouns and active verbs to those sense equivalents (eye, ear, nose, mouth, touch), you also solicit metaphor to coax more meaning out of their lair.

Kathleen Norris's *Dakota: A Spiritual Geography* is full of expressive detail amplified often with metaphor and simile.[7] The memoir tells of Norris's move from New York City to western South Dakota, cultural and geographical opposites. There, reconnecting to her childhood home and faith, Presbyterianism (she also becomes an oblate at a nearby Benedictine monastery), she discovers that the flat, and isolated, and farm-abandoned Dakota outland hides its allures in abundant yet starkly proportioned "small things, like grasshoppers in their samurai armor clicking and jumping as you pass" (156).

Noticing small things means noticing the nearby larger things as well—to know them is to name them. The land is "full of grasses: sedges, switch grass, needlegrass, wheatgrass" (156). To see the grasses, she has to stop, look, study. They are not labeled on white identity markers. Then she sees that what's close up is over-matched by what's afar. Most people, Norris observes, measure the Dakotas by one encompassing insight: "Look how far you can see!" Which is to say, the epiphanic available on the Plains pinpoints in its vastness not only the animal and plant kingdoms, but, more important, "the seemingly insignificant detail for what it is" (135). A diviner of sorts, Norris apprehends detail as significant because of its seeming insignificance.

How does she do this?

One night, after donating her grandmother's piano to a church and celebrating the gift with her friend Rita over a bottle of dandelion wine, Norris writes, "I began to hear that piano as Rita poured the wine. The dandelions spun around, glad to be yellow again, glad to be free of the dark" (135). The dandelion is a mere weed, but as wine the plant savors human companionship. What's more, as metaphor, the yellow is the ripening wheat of the Plains, the trapped wine in the bottle, the dark, urban East. And yes, Norris, too, escaped from Gotham's darkness, is glad to be free, home, and rerooted.

This complex trope—layered with piano, dandelion wine, and darkness—allows Norris and her readers to experience the land's complex uniformity. Her metaphor of uniformity is intricate and subtle. For example, "A person is forced inward," she writes, "by the sparseness of what is outward and visible in all this land and sky. The beauty of the Plains is like that of an icon; it does not give an inch to sentiment or romance. . . . Maybe seeing the Plains is like seeing an icon: what seems stern and almost empty is merely open, a door into some simple and holy state" (157).

What is Norris attempting, what are *you* attempting, by writing spiritually? Will the darkness light up because you marry detail and metaphor to coax the known animals out of the woods? Or do you find in the detail and the metaphor whole new species in the liminal forest? In other words, an attuned soul is not enough. Physical objects carry undiscovered meanings, but only after we probe their figurations fully.

Moreover, note above Norris's multiple qualifiers, which probably slipped past you. The beauty of seeing the Plains is *like* seeing an icon, which is rendered with noncommittal words—maybe, seems, almost, merely, some. Obviously, a few objects remain in what's "almost empty." Though indefinite, they're still there. Being convinced by what is not exactly definite yet present is a kind of accuracy we seek with spiritual memoir. *Almost definite* mirrors the fickleness of the spirit.

You may have left the city for the country once the city buried you and your spirituality. But coming home, you saddle the writing, oh trusty steed, oh stalwart mare, and ride into the flat beyond. But nothing's as simple as that. Writing sows just as much confusion as it does ah-ha, especially when "what seems stern and almost empty" belabors the confusion. None of these details and metaphors arrive in a box from Amazon. I'm sure Norris was more surprised than relieved to have found them manifesting in the good earth and awaiting her notice. Such discovery was the way she mapped this spiritual geography into being.

(5) *Generally, the spiritual writer works from two perspectives. The first centers on a narrative plot and its redemptive goal. The second centers on an essay-like staying-in-place and its assessing goal. Both carry untold potential. But the first is favored over the second and takes up much more room (see Mary Karr). A great-shakes adventure wins most bets, and hearts. But, wonder of wonders, among elastic writers, it is possible for the second strategy to be lesser in amount and greater in import.*

In most spiritual memoir, you have the narrator simply *doing* things, that is, showing us her efforts, tortuous and valiant, to reach her goal. Peter Matthiessen stops along the way more often than Cheryl Strayed does—to reflect in the present—but both reach the finish line. In a few uncommon books, you have the writer *assessing* things, that is, making a very big deal out of her self-realizations and larger meanings as she goes. This laddered-to plateau is often so satisfying that there's nothing to do but linger at the lookout.

To be clear: I'm not saying you ditch a swashbuckling story. By all means, err on the side of a frothy adventure over reminiscing about an inner Waterloo. But if you avoid the strategy of assessing, your time in the evanescent ether will seem just plain ordinary. In the hands of a deft, serene, and wise writer, our interiority is often ripe for extensive curiosity, philosophical or otherwise. And curiosity may have a redemptive plot of its own to unfold. There's room to assess. When the river is wide, it just flows more slowly.

Mary Rose O'Reilley, with two fine memoirs under her belt, stretches herself in and out of meditative spaces like no one else; she is among the most complexly drawn and rhetorically inquisitive writers you'll find essaying on being-in-place. The title of her 2000 book sounds its unstable warning: *The Barn at the End of the World: The Apprenticeship of a Quaker, Buddhist Shepherd.*[8] O'Reilley explores two occupations, tending sheep on a Minnesota farm—the travails of inoculating, shearing, lambing, and castrating, all here in rectum-cleansing detail—and several months of meditation and chore duty at the Buddhist retreat of Plum Village in France.

O'Reilley is not content with one religion; she's "omnivorous," devouring them all. Raised Catholic, two years a novitiate, later a Quaker, she earns a certificate in "spiritual direction" in her early fifties. She and her partner, empty-nesters, head to England to sing in a shape-note choir, and O'Reilley joins Thich Nhat Hanh at Plum Village, her head shaved for a few months of disciplined meditation and Dharma talks. She hopes her zigzagging palliates her frenetic nature: "I can worship just about anything that occupies a certain slant of light" (54), and "I seem to hear a whole chorus of conflicting voices in what I loosely call myself" (104).

Still, her desires run alongside her like a dog chasing car tires. O'Reilley the writer loves to shift moods as well as decades but often portrays herself sans self-esteem, which we see, au contraire, she possesses in spades. Patiently sweeping the barn one day, she notes playfully, "Thus I thought while trying to let go of thought, and then for one sweep of the broom I was not thinking" (60).

Like Annie Dillard, like Rilke, O'Reilley writes, "The spiritual life—or the writing life—depends above all on fidelity to objects" (95). Thus, her primary load is much ado about animal husbandry, home and abroad. There's less on her Buddhist practice, "which commends to us this relentless attention to nothing but the present" (86). She keeps trying to stay in that essayistic place, a slow-motion present. But even if she succeeds, it doesn't matter. The "story" here is O'Reilley measuring herself, more often than not, with the writer's reflective vigor. To wax a bit Zen on this: that writing which pushes her into and pulls her out of the porous in-between *is* the art's precision, a fulcrum—whatever she is pushed into, she pulls out of.

As though *any moment* is *every moment*, O'Reilley interrupts a one-horse anecdote with a careening, zip-here, zip-there, zip-elsewhere slide, motivated by her "blowzy, self-indulgent" self.

> Today we chant tunelessly after finishing meditation, a (to me) meaningless hymn about the bliss of dharma. It is more tedious than the Catholic masses of my childhood. At least the Gospels had some action, none of this "Listen, Ananda, form is emptiness, emptiness is form, form is not other than emptiness nor emptiness other than form." . . . Whenever someone starts to rant about darkness and the abyss, I start to dream of crème caramel, various shades of blue devoré velvet. My eyes fill with tears of self-pity, sensory deprivation, physical discomfort, and perfect confusion. (119)

I applaud such honesty in the narrator's character when sung with humor and sensuousness and sangfroid.

While the sheep-tending, shape-note singing, and barn-cleaning suggest the inconsequential, it's O'Reilley's skill at destabilizing her narrative and reflective choices that animates every experience no matter how tactile or exalted. Her worrisome assessment of herself is her story even though she grounds it in the grit of farm work. It's almost as if any immersion in the pool of "life lessons" prompts her restlessness. There's no getting over it; there's only getting into it.

Deciding how to emphasize which side of the doing/assessing equation is paramount. Not only is there no injunction that you tell your inner turmoil as a "spiritual story," but once you learn how to load your reflection with bite and inflammation (or humor and sensuousness), you can mire your memoirist's journey in doubts and worries and caprices and other grievances and still have readers think you are taking them somewhere *enlightening*.

(6) *The load of the memoir—that one element the author foregrounds above other elements—must be strong, incisive, and persuasive, earning the weightiness of the writer's insistence. Karr's load is agitated narrative; O'Reilley's load is agitated reflection. The tone of either, however, should never be so heavy-handed that the memoirist drowns her own authentic voice with that of the righteous.*

It's mostly a grim outing, reading Veronica Chater's *Waiting for the Apocalypse: A Memoir of Faith and Family*.[9] Her parents, who live under the self-imposed strictures of a fanatical Catholicism, make homelife agonizing for Veronica and her seven siblings. In the 1960s, the father rejects the heretical reforms of Vatican II, and the family rebels, opening storefront assemblies to hold, with other indignant outliers, the renegade Latin Mass, first in California, then Portugal. Wherever they go, they are unwelcome, and the isolation and family resentments prove calamitous. When Chater and her sister escape, which is often, they are caught and brought home, sullen and unforgiving of their father.

The story is piled to the rafters with Dad's daily lectures on hell's horrors and heaven's fantasies, papal infallibilities and teenage depravities, bordering on, if not outright, lunacy. Every rivet in the Catholic armor is rusted tight. You hear some of it in the sketch of Chater's mother, about whose complicity the author writes,

I doubt Mom ever had an explosion of faith. You don't have explosions without fuel and something to set it off. Mom is steady and non-volatile, even slightly bureaucratic about her faith. She's a loyal follower of protocol and very good at dealing with the logistics of religion—with its day-to-day disciplines, routines, words, rituals. But I don't know how much she *feels*. Mom would never mistakenly say the Joyful Mysteries on a Tuesday; or miss a Holy Day of Obligation; or forget a religious feast; or cook meat on Friday. . . . She does everything precisely as she learned, as if religion were a formula for getting to heaven, and each forgotten word or missed genuflection might dilute the strength of the portion needed to get there. But what does it all *mean* to her? (219–20)

With Mom indisposed and Dad whacked, Chater eventually has to parent herself, give to herself what's been denied her in childhood. Just before she escapes for good, she has a fateful fall out of a tree, trying to retrieve her pet parrot. The knock on the noggin revives her apostasy yet again, but this time her insights, as she tells her brother (who has come home after he was imprisoned in a South American Jesus camp), are furiously enumerated:

God isn't what we think. Death isn't what we think. Heaven and hell aren't what we think. What lies after death is unknowable. I'm no authority on what lies after it, but what I do know is that we're not going to burn for eternity. How do I know this? I don't know how I know. I just *know* that I *know*. Know what I mean? Just like I know how to ride a bicycle, or tie my shoes, or run. I can't explain how I know, only that *I know*. (310)

You get Chater's emphasis, her wild mind, turning the idea of faith on its head. She hasn't lost faith; she's identifying those instinctual beacons in her she can't help but be faithful to— intuition, native intelligence, predisposition, the sacred self inborn.

God for Chater has been, until this moment when she's seventeen, that which the old Catholic Church and her parents and a Christianly bent culture in America thinks God is. Not so. (Not so, of course, does not mean nothing. It means not what she's been taught.)

Curiously, though, this penultimate scene is not her liberation. Why? Because the "Catholic child," in the context of the "Catholic family," is already engorged, a Mississippi River of pre–Vatican II supremacist nonsense. To move on—if the writing will even allow it—she first must drain her own swamp. No one just surfaces from indoctrination and swims free, especially in a family of eight with parents who, for twenty years, begrudgingly shelter her, for the most part. The way out comes only via incremental forgiveness. Which is, wisely, the chief tone Chater employs.

Her tone isn't anti-family or anti-God. Nor is it one of joyful spiritual freedom or strident religious deconversion. The tone is respectful, even loyal, to her family, parents and siblings. Throughout, Chater pays homage to her siblings, who are clever but overmatched rebels. They practice a kind of group survival, nurturing one another's complaints, unwilling to bolt as that would leave the younger ones behind. Chater also pays homage, strangely, to her parents. In the end, they come out not as devils but as misled protectors. (To blame religion for their immaturity as parents is to avoid the question of individual character.) Chater portrays her love of Mom and Dad's absurdly ruinous love of Catholicism with as much wonder as anger.

Her compassionate tone, blending wonder and anger, is all grown up. Here is a narrator who is gentle on the adolescent's stockade and who is alarmed that the same girl withstood the doctrinal onslaught. And yet that alarm emerges rarely, though pointedly, because she keeps the reflective adult writer's incredulity and hurt both present and at bay.

Still, Chater's *Waiting for the Apocalypse* is ultimately a personal provocation for children to live free—at least, to have the right to live free—of parental brainwashing. It is a memoir about justice from a victim who cannot execute her jailers because she loves them. A Christian message from, I assume, an ex-Christian author.

(7) Trust and a resultant goodwill are the lifeblood of writing spiritually.

The degree to which the writer is trustworthy is one of those ongoing questions I ask every memoir I read. But the query seems more crucial for those authors with a spiritual bent. What's more crucial is also a harder nut to crack.

In memoir, we may or we may not trust the narrator, which, remember, is a *creation* (less generously, a *device*) of the writer. That narrator may be less reliable because he likes to pretend, use irony, dabble in the postmodern, exaggerate the rhetorically excessive. But if that's his route, we suppose his critical purpose and contradictory judgment require a manipulative teller. The spiritually minded narrator, however, is a creature who is bent by *and* must show his own need to manipulate the reader, splitting his personality—*what I am not yet, I am.* If he is too heavily or darkly masked, he strays into fiction and emerges like the confessor in Dostoevsky's *Notes from Underground,* who embodies unrelenting ennui and has lost to type his individuality. And yet using an eccentric or finessed teller doesn't mean the nonfictional aspect of a story is compromised.

To assess any teller, I ask questions. How fallible is he? Is there some blindness or accident that keeps him from telling the whole story? How would you know if he is hiding something or his work has ill intent? Is he too full of himself as hero or savior, as wounded healer, as absurdist, as nihilist? Contrarily, is he such a novice that he settles for a projection, a persona, a polemicist instead of an authentic ego? Might he dialogue persona and ego, which implies a literate intent? Does the narrator possess the verisimilitude or roundedness we prize from conscientious storytellers, the Robert Pirsigs of the world?[10]

I can further complicate the teller's character by returning to the basic premise of confessional autobiography. If the book claims—I'm thinking of Augustine's *Confessions* or John of the Cross's *Dark Night of the Soul*—to represent how each man has been reborn, why should we believe it? Because it's "based on a true story"? Why believe the Buddha, when no YouTube video verifies his existence, let alone his experience, forty-nine days under the bodhi tree to get enlightened? Given the necessarily unverifiable stories of those we want to trust, those we assume have no reason to lie like Mother Teresa, we should be *more*, not *less* wary of every teller. Her unreliability is inescapable. Moreover, we can't let sincerity—as in the trendy phrase "sincerely held religious belief"—be the yardstick.

After all, we're contending with the inscrutability of Jehovah, visions of Mother Mary, and psychic walls to Nirvana, any of whose substance must be "taken on faith" or is couched as "indescribable." That last word widens the gap between the grit of revelation and the inequivalence of language. Every writer who works into or out of faith trades in the import/export business of unreliability. Consider these inconclusive warrants: thirty years ago, my brother molested me; on his deathbed, my father told me I was his favorite child; in my last past life, I was a Salem witch. The more unverifiable the claim, the more (potentially) unreliable the narrator is. Because we ourselves are so often dubious about our transcendent nature, we feel religious/spiritual assertions in writing from sage or simpleton cannot be *anything but unreliable*.

A narrator is trustworthy when, despite his innocence, his naïveté, youth, or immaturity, a mature voice contextualizes that innocence. A narrator is trustworthy when he shows sensitivity for others and their points of view. He is trustworthy when he presents the religious, spiritual, or nonaffiliated family or community that has steeped him in what he believes or disbelieves. He is trustworthy when he places his vulnerabilities on a par with his self-esteem. He is trustworthy when his writing is rigorously literate, using the very elements I'm here describing. And he is trustworthy when he holds himself accountable for his despair or his insight and shows us how it affects or changes the way he thinks, feels, and writes.

One stabilizing trick is to contrast the self-consciousness the narrator presents with the altered or new person he has awakened to. It is also possible for a writer to reroute a narrator's story to achieve a higher end, say, keeping the spiritual discovery from ossifying into a creed. When a kind of enigmatic narration rules, you trust the narrator because the writer has given him the desire, even the will, to be reformed or redeemed or to remain lost. Our trust in a narrator who excavates and interlayers these perspectives cannot help but generate goodwill toward both the teller and the tale.

(8) *Whatever you enlist the spirit to help you say is far different from what you do say once you start working the craft of writing to your transformative advantage.*

Thomas Merton is the oddest and the most undeniably spiritual of authors. In another letter from him to Étienne Gilson (I quoted one at the beginning of this book), the Cistercian monk writes, "In none of the books that I have written do I feel that I have said what I wanted."[11] We might take this aggravation at face value: what he says he means *is* what he means, roughened by an ominous tone, which any fool can hear. He sounds convinced that he failed to find whatever it was he thought was the point or the idea of the book which he set out to write.

But because it's Merton asserting himself—note the bravura, the succinctness, and the four ball-peened accents on "I"—there are other interpretations of the sentence than what appears obvious.

Such as: In the books Merton has written, what he ends up saying is what the writing needed to say, perhaps on his behalf, perhaps to challenge him or wake him up, perhaps to remind him how much he had censored himself or the church would do it for him, stopped his renegade thoughts and querulous feelings from going too far in any one direction—all conditions that led him away from or burrowed under what he wanted to say.

Take this to the bank: You can never write spiritually if the writing you do is done to say what you want to say, which is seldom if ever what you were going to say, because when or if the spirit shows up, it has any number of deviations in store for you, as it has already revealed to other writers before you, and, like them, you have little or no idea what those deviations are, so you do the only thing you can do, which is to get the writing going and get yourself out of the way so that when or if the spirit shows up, in whatever disguise it chooses, which you'll get good at spotting over time, only then does the journey begin.

NOTES

1. Mary Karr, *Lit* (New York: Harper Perennial, 2009).

2. Chet Raymo, *When God Is Gone, Everything Is Holy: The Making of a Religious Naturalist* (Norte Dame, IN: Sorin Books, 2008).

3. Beverly Donofrio, *Looking for Mary: Or, The Blessed Mother and Me* (New York: Penguin Books, 2000).

4. For example. This book began as an essay trying to describe the nature of a holy book, then became a book-length argument about why much of the Bible fails as literature, then became a book about the growing generation of unbelievers in America we call Nones, and then, digging deeper, found its present voice in linking spirituality and the writer.

Some who may wish to know: I have not been converted to any religion—nor do I think I will be—but I have suffered a conversion of sorts, a knowingness or, better, a being-ness, about the narrative and rhetorical verve of the spiritual writers I cover in this book. I had no idea before I read them what each had deemed so difficult, nearly impossible, to write about and then went ahead and did it anyway.

5. Quoted in Christopher Hitchens, *The Missionary Position: Mother Teresa in Theory and Practice* (New York: Verso, 1995), 82.

6. Mother Teresa, *Come Be My Light: The Private Writings of the "Saint of Calcutta,"* ed. Brian Kolodiejchuck (New York: Doubleday, 2007).

7. Kathleen Norris, *Dakota: A Spiritual Geography* (New York: Houghton Mifflin, 1993).

8. Mary Rose O'Reilley, *The Barn at the End of the World: The Apprenticeship of a Quaker, Buddhist Shepherd* (Minneapolis: Milkweed Editions).

9. Veronica Chater, *Waiting for the Apocalypse: A Memoir of Faith and Family* (New York: W. W. Norton, 2009).

10. For this analysis of narrator traits, I'm indebted to *The Bedford Glossary of Critical and Literary Terms*, ed. Ross Murfin and Supryia M. Ray (Boston: Bedford Books, 1997), 232–33.

11. *Echoing Silence: Thomas Merton on the Vocation of Writing*, ed. Robert Inchausti (Boston: New Seeds, 2007), 165.